Sue's Story

SUE OWEN

Sue's Story

HOW I SURVIVED
A LOST CHILDHOOD

metro

Published by Metro Publishing Ltd,
3, Bramber Court, 2 Bramber Road,
London W14 9PB, England

www.blake.co.uk

First published in hardback in 2005

ISBN 1 84358 144 2

British Library Cataloguing-in-Publication Data:

A catalogue record for this book is available from the British Library.

Design by www.envydesign.co.uk

Printed in Great Britain by Creative Print & Design (Wales)

1 3 5 7 9 10 8 6 4 2

Papers used by Metro Publishing are natural, recyclable products made from wood grown in sustainable forests. The manufacturing processes conform to the environmental regulations of the country of origin.

All photographs from the author's collection.

Zebras have to stay in their herds. One zebra gave birth but her baby injured his leg. Mum tried desperately to get the rest of the herd to slow down but in the end she had to leave her baby behind, probably to be savaged and eaten by the hyenas that were closing in. The baby could walk no longer, the rest of the herd walked on. The mother knew that she had to keep with the rest of the herd, for her own safety, and so she said goodbye to her baby.

A few days later her baby rejoined the group, his leg had recovered and he had managed to run off from any would-be predators.

He went happily back to the mother, the one who had left him for dead.

To my husband Darren and my son and daughter,
whose strength, support and love have helped me make it
through the tough times. I love you all.

The aggravating features of this case are clear: this was prolonged and sustained sexual abuse and the victim of it was your own daughter, someone who looked to you for protection. This was a gross abuse of trust in your position as her father. The sentences that I pass upon you today must reflect the revulsion that the public feels about this type of conduct.

The sentences total six years' imprisonment. On each count you will go to prison for a period of twelve months, but these sentences will run consecutively to one another, making six in all.

In addition, I order that you sign the Sex Offenders Register.

EXTRACT FROM SENTENCING REPORT, 2 NOVEMBER 2001

FOREWORD

It is now eight months later and I'm still very mixed up. In one way I'm relieved that my abuser has been severely punished, but then again it is my dad! I have thought non-stop about him and the rest of the family. There's one rule I try to live by and that is quite simply: 'Don't do to others what you wouldn't like done to you.' I couldn't imagine life in prison and hopefully I will never have to experience it. I still feel responsible for him being there – why could I not just forgive him? But he never asked to be forgiven, and he wouldn't admit to doing anything wrong. I don't know how he's coping in there, for he's such a weak man.

The last phone call I had from my brother was just after the first court case. I was letting him know that I was keen on going to the press to share my story. I felt that, if I had known that there were many other people like me out there, I might have sought help a lot sooner. He said, 'You've got what you want, just let it go.' I didn't get what I wanted. I wanted my dad to say, 'Sorry, I was wrong. I shouldn't have done that to you.' I would have liked it if he had said that he felt bad about what he'd done. He didn't. He saw it as acceptable.

I would like to say that I did it to prevent any other little girls from going through what I went through. But I didn't. I did it because I know that I shouldn't have been treated like that. Even though I still find it hard to associate me with that little girl, I really did it for her. There is wrong and there is right, but sometimes the wrong is just too wrong.

Tonight I was cooking the evening meal and again I thought about him. What is he eating? Is he getting bullied? Is he in solitary? Other people tell me to just forget him as he got what he deserved, but it isn't easy. When I was a little girl I used to look forward to him coming home, as my stepmother was never nasty to me in front of him. I think that's what makes this worse — it's like I preferred his abuse, but at the time I didn't know it was wrong; I was just relieved that I wasn't receiving a belting.

I do miss my family. I am deeply hurt by the fact that some of them know the truth but have totally denied it. Others, after being told, just assumed that I was lying.

My sister told me, 'It's not that I don't believe you, it's just that I don't want to.'

As for my stepmother, I'm still trying to find the answer. I'm very angry that she has escaped doing time in prison. I still ask myself, What was the point?

ONE

My earliest memory is of lying in a double bed with two of my three brothers, Andrew and Paul. Anthony had a bed on the other wall. Normally I had the boxroom, but my dad had been sleeping in there for a while. He was married to Deidre, with a two-year-old and a newborn son when he had an affair with my mother Kathleen. When I was born, I lived with my stepmother Deidre, my father Allan and my three half-brothers. Mum, as I called my stepmother then, of course, sat on Anthony's bed and was going to read us a story when she turned to me and said, 'Not you. Turn over and go to sleep.'

I was never allowed to join in with them in anything. I managed to see the book the next day when the boys had gone to school. I wasn't old enough to go to school and couldn't yet read, so I just looked at the pictures.

We lived in a three-bedroom house in a respectable area just outside London. My father had many jobs. He started out as a policeman; not just an ordinary PC but a City of London one.

1

I didn't really know what the difference was but it just sounded more important. He went on to become a milkman, a potato-delivery man and a lorry driver. It was the *sssshhhh* from his lorry that I used to look forward to hearing; it would be the one and only reason that I dared to leave my bed, just to see if he was returning home.

A lot of my early life I spent alone in my small room. Normally I would come home from school and Mum would scream at me to go up to bed. After the family had eaten their meal I was called down to wash up but unless my father was there she rarely offered me a meal. My brothers and I took it in turns to do the meal jobs. I always washed up, but we would take it in turns to dry up, put away, lay and clear the table. Every morning I would dust and polish and the boys took it in turns to hoover.

School holidays were a little better as I was allowed out and also I ate at the table with the others. I don't know if that was a good thing or not as my stepmother had some strict table rules. Sometimes I knew I had to be punished as I had been bad, but other times I just didn't have a clue what I'd done.

My school was only ten minutes' walk down the road. I never rushed home; there was no point as I'd only have to go to my room. My little boxroom was at the front of the house, my parents' room was next to mine, then my brothers' room and finally the bathroom. I hated Fridays as I never knew what the weekend would entail. Would I be allowed out? Or would it be a boring, hungry one spent in my room? Sometimes when I arrived home, before I could even open my mouth, Mum would say, 'Bed!'

A few times I had been allowed to stay up. Thursdays were a

good day as my nan used to visit, but she would only stay until 4.30. Still, an hour was better than nothing. Whenever my dad was home I was allowed to stay up, for my mum was never horrible to me in front of him. I loved it when he was there.

I remember one day arriving home from school feeling very hungry. Salad had been the school dinner that day and I hated it because it never filled me up. I was sent to bed as usual. When my mum called me down to do the dishes, I was hoping to grab some leftovers from the boys' plates, but all that was left was fatty bits of meat on Paul's plate. So I remained hungry. I thought about the biscuit tin, but I remembered once sneaking into it and it had a noisy lid, which Mum heard, so I got a beating for being a thief. I was already a 'slut's child', a 'waste of space', an 'ugly little spawny shitface', lucky to be living with her. I also stole some uncooked spaghetti once, but as I couldn't chew it very quickly it made me choke, which she heard. I got a beating while I was choking. 'That'll teach you,' she said. And it did. I never stole spaghetti again.

I had always known that I wasn't her 'proper' child. The story was that my mother was going to come and get me on a Saturday afternoon when I was a few weeks old, but she never turned up. My stepmother had no choice but to hang on to me. I had always known that I had an older sister called Alice who was kept by my real mum. I don't remember ever being told; it was just something that I had always known. Same as my name isn't Susan: it's Jennifer, Jennifer Doonie, or 'Loonie', as my brothers used to tease me.

So I finished the dishes and went up to bed hungry. But I had a plan. I was going to sneak downstairs when everyone was in bed and get some food. What should I have? Biscuits? No! Noisy lid. Bread? No! Crinkly bag. Weetabix? No! Too messy and very hard to swallow (I had tried before). Some cheese? No! That would have meant using a knife to cut it. That was the end of my plan: we hadn't any food easy enough for me to steal.

There was a lamppost outside my window and when it came on I would count the seconds until the next one up the hill came on. That's it, the fun and games were over. Time for sleep. I hadn't a clock in my room, just a bed, a cupboard and my windowsill. I didn't have any books or toys because I was told that I was bad and so didn't deserve any. As soon as the streetlights came on I would settle down to sleep. Sometimes I would drop off but would be woken up by the boys coming to bed. They were allowed to be noisy and have fun. Sometimes I would lie there trying to get to sleep but couldn't because I needed to go to the toilet and didn't dare leave my room. Not until the boys were in bed and all was quiet would I risk leaving my bedroom.

I awoke one day, made my bed, got dressed and went downstairs to do my dusting and polishing. Mum was still in bed, so I got a bowl and had two pieces of Shredded Wheat, which I ate very quickly. No one else was up yet and I was just thinking about having another two when I heard her coughing. I wasn't going to push my luck – at least I'd had two. She came down, didn't even look at me and said, 'Bed!' I ran upstairs crying as I'd really hoped that I would be allowed out. I hated going to bed on Saturdays as it was such a long day. I heard the front door slam and I took a look out of my window, crouching down in case anyone was looking up. I saw Mum had gone out with the boys and I really wished I could be with them.

Being in my bedroom was so boring. Sometimes I'd sneak books in to read. I had always loved Enid Blyton and used to pray that I could somehow be sent to St Clare's or Malory Towers. I wouldn't even mind if I didn't go home during the holidays. I was always scared in case Mum found them and tore them up. I once wrote a story and was given a gold star. I had to stand up in class and everyone applauded me, but she found it and tore it up. Why? I don't know. I was scared to take things home after that and nearly cried after my teacher said, 'This year you'll start getting homework.'

Today, however, I don't know whether I was angry for being sent to bed that day. I felt brave. I went downstairs and sat in the armchair. Wow! I felt so grown up as we children sat only on the settee or floor. I went round the room. She had a box of Matchmakers on a shelf – I had seen them there while I was dusting earlier – so I sat in the armchair and ate some. I shook the box so no one would notice any missing. As I was putting them back on the shelf I looked up and saw them all returning, so I flew upstairs, hoping and praying they didn't see me.

But they did. My brother told me that through our glass door they all saw me running up the stairs with my bare bottom showing under my nightie. I jumped into bed and pretended to be asleep, but she burst in, grabbed me, demanded where I'd been and beat me. At the time her beatings were just slaps, punches and kicks. I hated the slaps most as they really stung.

After that incident Mum started putting down talc outside my door, so that when she was out she would know if I'd got out of my room. I only knew it was there as I had to hoover it up once she'd returned. I never dared leave my room again without permission. I had learned my lesson. At the time I felt I deserved the beating as I'd left my room when she had told me not to. I had been bad.

I hated the nights; they seemed so long. Sometimes when everyone was in bed I'd go into the bathroom and take a swig of Night Nurse as it 'aids restful sleep'. Even when I was asleep at night, I could still be abused by them, both sexually and physically. On awaking, the first thing I would find out was who was there by my bed. If it was Dad, 'Phew, relief', it was OK, because I was safe with him; he had told me many times that he loved me. If it was her, I'd start begging her forgiveness for whatever it was I had done wrong.

TWO

Occasionally family friends would come over. I was allowed to get up for these evenings. Dave Johnson was my dad's friend and they would sit in the front room drinking and smoking. His wife was her friend and they would stay in the sitting room smoking and drinking, while my brothers and I would play with their two boys. Outside we mainly played One Two Three Homey. We had a base, our gatepost, and one person was the finder while the rest hid. When someone was seen they would try to run to the base before the finder caught them. I loved playing that.

There was a synagogue nearby and it was always a good place to hide. The only problem was Andrew. If I caught him, he would always deny it and tell her that I was cheating. She would tell me off so sweetly in front of everyone, but when no one was looking she would give me 'the look' and then I knew I was going to get it later on.

So I gave up playing outside with my brothers and stayed in

with a pack of cards. I would stand two cards up and rest them on each other. These were my little castles. Or I would put three on the bottom, balance two on top and then, with a very steady hand, balance another on top: my pyramids. But Paul, the Johnsons' eldest boy, thought it was immensely funny to bang his foot on the floor, causing my little castles and pyramids to come crashing down. I couldn't complain, though, as at least I had spent the evening out of my room and I did enjoy making my buildings. If I was feeling very adventurous I would make lots of two-card castles in a long line and then tap the first one and watch it fall on to the next one and that would fall on to its neighbour and so on. I loved playing with my cards and wished that I could sneak them into my bedroom. I would never be bored again.

Of my brothers I hated Andrew the most. Generally they left me alone, though sometimes they taunted me by calling me Loonie, Vincent or Van Gogh. I knew where the first nickname came from, but the other two I didn't have a clue about. Andrew was a bully-boy: his favourite joke was to throw glass jars at me. If I didn't catch them, obviously they would break all over the floor and I would get a beating. He just used to stand there smiling.

Another thing he liked to do was soak the end of a tea towel and then flick it at me so that the wet end would sting me. I swore to myself that when I was older I would never have anything to do with him. At the time I was probably closest to Paul as he was nearest to me in age and we both went to the same school. Anthony was the kindest and quietest of the three; he used to try to sneak food in to me when I had to stay in my bedroom.

Mum was friendly with the Evans family, who lived over the road. Margaret Evans had five boys. Three of them were grown up and the youngest two were at high school. I liked Margaret as she was kind and often helped me with my speech problems. I used to stutter quite badly and there were many words I couldn't pronounce. Over and over she would repeat the words, then get me to say them. Her youngest boy, Philip, was just a little older than my brothers and we often played together. Whenever we had guests Mum was a different person towards me. She was kind, she laughed, she called me Susie and everyone thought she was a super mum. It was only when she flashed me 'the look' that I knew it was still her. But I still enjoyed those days.

Sundays were sometimes good days as my dad never worked then. I was allowed out in the mornings and would go and play with friends. Dinner was at one o'clock: a roast. After washing up I was allowed out again but not allowed to play with friends as Sunday afternoons were a time for parents to have a nap in their armchairs. So I used to walk round the streets picking up ring-pulls to give to the church. Greenford Broadway was always a good place to get loads; sometimes my pockets would bulge, they were so full. It was so much better than staying in my room.

One Sunday I woke up to be told one of our kittens was missing. I hadn't even known that our cat was pregnant, let alone had given birth. The kittens were so cute. We all had to search the house until the missing one was found. I went into my brothers' room and noticed how windy it was outside. All the washing, not just in our garden but in all the neighbouring gardens, was trying desperately to stay pegged on to the lines. I so wanted to find the kitten before it could get out, for I felt sure it would be blown away. We had a porch at the front of our house and I looked in there. I looked in the shoe cupboard inside the porch. No, it wasn't there. As I was closing the porch door I was wondering where to look next when suddenly I felt a pain in my head.

Mum was cooking the Sunday roast and so I went to find Anthony to tell him that I'd hurt my head. He looked at me and told me to go and tell her. 'Oh, my God!' she yelled when she saw me. My head was pouring blood. Apparently, when I opened the porch door, the handle sliced into the top of my head. Mum called my dad down, cleaned me up and then he took me to the hospital. We didn't have a car, so we had to go by bus. As it was a Sunday we had to wait ages, with me standing there holding a towel to my head. I was told I needed stitches and the doctor said it might hurt a bit, but it didn't. I just sat there while they did it and then went home. Being Sunday, it was bath and hair-wash day, but I couldn't have either. The only other time I had ever missed my Sunday-night bath was when my leg had got a cigarette burn. It stung so much when I put it in the water that my mum had to take me out in case my dad heard my screams.

When I went to school the next day I had to give my teacher a letter saying I wasn't to be allowed out at playtime or to do any gym. I was so disappointed, but the teacher got me a grown-up chair that I was allowed to sit on during story and milk time, instead of on the floor. I felt so important. I loved all my teachers in first school. I loved school. On school mornings

I was out of the door at 8.15. On my ten-minute walk each day I used to see a woman taking her children to the Catholic school. The two girls looked happy and were always smiling. I would be happy too, I thought, if I had a nice mum who took me to school every day. I also saw another woman on the other side of the road, who would take her son halfway there and then watch him for the other half.

Like me, Paul was still at the first school, but Anthony and Andrew were at the middle school, which was opposite. Sometimes after school I would walk in the front door and sense straight away that there was going to be trouble. One day Mum called me in and said, 'What have you been doing today?'

'Nothing.'

'Get here.'

I had to stand within smacking range. My stomach started to get all knotty.

Smack! She got me right across my face. I hated the smacks. My body had got used to the punches and kicks, but not the smacks. She raised her hand so high that I was more scared than I was worried about the actual pain.

'I'll ask you again. What have you been doing?'

'I don't know.' As soon as I said that I wished I hadn't. She hated it and it just seemed to get her more angry.

'I know what you've been doing, so you might as well just tell me. Well?'

'I didn't do anything.' I tried to find the answers to her questions but sometimes I would just completely run out of answers.

Smack! Smack! She got me on both sides of the face.

'You were playing football, weren't you?' Seven-year-old girls weren't allowed to play football.

'No, I wasn't.' My thoughts raced back to dinnertime, when I had been standing by the fence, but I wasn't in goal as the boys were using the next fence down as their goal.

'So you're saying that I'm lying?'

Smack.

'Get back here!' I had moved an inch away every time she struck me.

'I know everything you do!'

This was true. At playtime skipping ropes and small plastic balls were thrown about the playground so that the children could pick them up to play with. There weren't enough for everybody. Mum told me that I was never allowed to play with them because, if I did, it would mean that a nice, proper girl was missing out. One day I had to throw the balls and ropes around the playground. Mum had thought I was playing with them and so I got a beating. I was once asked to jump in the rope while my friend was skipping. I thought this would be OK, as I wasn't actually touching it. But it wasn't. Every single thing that I had done, my mum got to know about. I used to imagine that the two mothers I passed every day were her spies. The lollipop lady was also in with her and so were the dinner ladies. I even stopped talking to my friends just in case they went home and told their mums and they then told her. I looked at her.

'I wasn't playing football, Mummy.'

'Show me your fingers.'

That was it, she'd got me. I had been a nail biter all my life and it had got so bad that I used to nibble at the skin at the sides until my fingers were red raw. I held out my hands for her to inspect. She looked at them and left the room. I knew all too well what was coming next. She returned with her little bowl of mixture. I didn't know the exact contents but vinegar was a major ingredient. I started crying and promised her I would never bite them again. She sat down at the table.

'Get here.'

'Please. I promise.'

At times like this I pleaded with her, but she never took any notice. Sometimes it was like she'd never even heard me. She would take my hand and force my fingers into the bowl, even giving them a little swish around just to make sure that she'd not missed a bit. My body would leap into the air and my arm didn't follow only because she was holding my hand tight in the bowl. She never left them in there for too long, for once all the sores were covered the stinging eased. She would do the other hand as well and tears would stream down my face, but she never took any notice of them.

After the 'punishment' I was always allowed to go to bed. Most of the time I hated being sent to bed, but this time I was so relieved that I was out of her way. I flew up the stairs, blowing on my fingers, which were still on fire. Why didn't I do as I was told? Why did I disobey her and still keep on biting my fingernails? If I had been good, things would have been a lot better.

THREE

One morning I woke dressed, washed, cleaned my shoes – I always had to be clean and smart – dusted and polished and then ate my breakfast. Then I asked Mum if I could leave for school but she said no. She was in a good mood and said that I could stay at home and we would go shopping. I was over the moon. She made me tomato soup for dinner and I was even allowed to have some bread with it, which I was allowed to dip in! After dinner she said that it was too late to go shopping. I was a little disappointed but at least we were having a good day. As I was eating my soup I looked out of the window and noticed Mrs Smith, our school welfare lady, walking past. I told Mum that it was lucky that we hadn't gone shopping as she would have seen us and known that I wasn't ill. All the time I knew that, even though Mum was being nice, she would want me to do something for her in return. She was never good to me without a reason.

I got home from school one day and my dad was home, so

I was allowed to stay up. But sometimes he went back out and as soon as he was out of the door I was sent to bed. That day I was watching TV and all I could think was, Please, Dad, don't go out until *Paddington Bear* is over. It was coming on at 5.35 and I really wanted to watch it. At 5.05 – the time was going too slowly – there was some boring programme on. Mum and Dad were in the kitchen. I don't know where the boys were. It got to 5.35 and *Paddington Bear* was coming on just as Mum came in and kicked me in the chest. I had no chance to prepare for it and so it really hurt. I couldn't breathe. She told me to shut up and not to dare cry in front of my father. Tears stopped coming out of my eyes but my stomach wouldn't stop trembling. I don't know why she did it. Lots of things were now happening and I didn't know what I had done.

I decided that I was going to run away. I had done this a few times already but had gone back home when darkness fell. This time, though, I was going for good. And I didn't care if they caught me and put me in a home for bad girls. This is what Mum told me would happen, and that would mean everyone would know that I was bad. I spent the rest of the day in my room. Anthony couldn't get me any food; he was too scared to because Mum was in a foul mood.

I woke the next day, did my jobs and went to school. Mum stayed in bed that morning. Dinnertime came and it was my favourite, roast lamb. The dinner ladies used to laugh at me, as I was always up for seconds and thirds of whatever they had going, though I was still very skinny. 'Lamppost' and 'Beanpole', my friends called me.

Three-thirty came and I set off for Horsenden Hill. I didn't really know how to get there but it turned out to be very easy: straight up the Greenford Road. The Grand Union canal runs by the hill and I sat beside it throwing stones in. I couldn't go up the hill as it was getting dark and I was beginning to get scared. I looked at the canal and had a brilliant idea. I would go back to Greenford and go to Perivale Park, walk along the side of the River Brent, which would then take me on to the Thames, which then leads to the seaside. I had seen it in Geography in school. The only snag was that when I got there it was pitch-dark and I was just too scared to walk into Perivale Park to get to the river. I felt it must have been about ten o'clock and I started realising that if I saw a police car I'd have to hide as they'd probably be out looking for me now.

I went through the car park, which led to Ravenor Park, from where I could see my house. My dad's lorry wasn't there, which meant he wasn't home yet. I was bored. They must surely have missed me by now. I was cold as well, so I went home. It was always fun planning to run away, but it was quite boring actually doing it. I knocked at the door and went in. Mum was lying on the settee watching telly.

'Where you been?'

'Just walking around,' I replied.

'Picking up them bloody shitty can rings, I suppose. Go on, get up to bed.' And that was that. No police searches, no 'missing girl' headlines and my mum wasn't crying all over me, saying how worried she had been. Still at least I got out for the evening.

Summer holidays were good as I got to go out a lot more. I would visit some of my school friends. One of them, Sandra, had every single one of the Famous Five books, which she used to lend me. I was too scared to take them home in case my mum ripped them up, so I sat in the park and read them, then took them straight back. I did have a Bay City Rollers school bag but my mum tore it up in front of me, and I then had to tell my dad that it was me who had done it.

Unfortunately, she had her summer punishment where she would make me stand in the garden facing the wall (so she didn't have to see my face) with my hands on top of my head. I always remember how my elbows and backs of my legs would hurt for days. It hurt to straighten my arms and it also hurt bending my legs.

It was my birthday in July and one year I got two tennis rackets. I used to play tennis with Sandra but that didn't last long as Mum got angry and snapped my rackets in half. But I still had fun with my friends. If they weren't in I'd go collecting my can rings. I'd also go blackberry picking for Mum, so she could make puddings with them. I would leave the house with my empty ice-cream container and not return until it was full. I was very scared of spiders and there were sometimes the biggest ones ever, with the longest legs, in my blackberry bushes. But I would still pick my blackberries. I wanted so much to see my mum's look of delight when she looked in the container I brought her and saw that it was full.

Everyone loved my mum's blackberry pies or crumbles, which made me feel good. The only downside to blackberries was that they stained our pudding bowls (beetroot was also a nightmare to clean). Teatime was sometimes fine and I enjoyed being there. But most of the time it was very painful. Mum kept a metal serving spoon close to her plate and, if I did something that was considered bad manners, I would get hit on the knuckles with it. Twenty-six times I had to chew each mouthful of food.

'Don't put food into your mouth until you finish what is in there,' she would say.

I hated that spoon. She would always get me on the knuckles. As it was summertime we had salad a lot. I don't really like salad because you can't really chew it 26 times without it disappearing. One time I put my hand on the salad-cream bottle.

Whack.

'Ask, don't help yourself.'

'Please may I have some salad cream?' I asked, trying to keep the tears under control.

'No, that's for not asking the first time.'

Whack.

'Don't look at me, look at what's on your own plate.'

Whack.

'Sit up. Don't let your hair fall into your food.'

The boys were there but I didn't see or hear them as I was too busy concentrating on chewing 26 times, sitting with my head up, eyes down and trying not to cry, for if I did my nose would run and I'd get a whack for sniffing. We all had a cup of tea afterwards. I was considered a weird child because I didn't like tea. Apparently it wasn't normal to dislike it, so I had to drink it all. I wasn't allowed to leave until the whole lot had gone. I would wait for it to go cold and then drink it down in one gulp.

For me the worst meal was spaghetti bolognese. I'll always remember the feeling of total dread whenever I saw the table laid with forks and spoons. The whole meal was constant whacks, mainly for being messy. The boys were allowed to suck their spaghetti up and make loads of mess, but not me. I longed for the meal to be over. All those nights when I had been in my bedroom, listening to them having their tea and wishing I could be there. Now I was there and I was wishing that I could be back up in my bedroom. If I did manage to get some food up to mouth without making any mess, I then had to chew it and keep on chewing it.

Whack.

'Don't you swallow it yet. That wasn't 26 times.'

Mum would even watch my throat movements. I couldn't wait for the holidays to be over. Corn on the cob was also a nightmare as it was impossible to eat it without making any mess.

Sometimes my nan would come over to spend the evening with us. She was actually my dad's nan and had raised him from a young age as his mother died just after the war. I felt so sorry for him when I found out that his mum had died. One evening Mum was not in a good mood before Nan came, and before she arrived she had a little talk with me. Grabbing my hair, she said, 'You listen to me, shitface, you'd better not come into the sitting room with us tonight and don't even think about asking to watch *Top of the Pops*.'

'Yes, Mum.'

After the meal I did the dishes while Mum, Nan and the boys were watching TV. I didn't know what to do next. Do I go upstairs to bed? Do I stay in the kitchen? What?

'Mum, can I come in now, please?' I said, going into the sitting room.

'Now, Susie, remember what we talked about earlier.'

I went out and shut the door. What should I say to Nan? Do I say, 'Goodnight'? Or just go upstairs? Would I be in trouble for ignoring her? Again I didn't know. Mum came into the kitchen after me and shut the door behind her. I was going to ask her what I should say to my nan but her face was black. I was scared. She thumped and slapped me. I fell to the floor and she kicked me, then pulled me up by my hair. She had her hands around my throat and was strangling me. She'd never done that before. I was very scared now. When I fell to the floor again she continued to kick me.

'That'll teach you to disobey me. Now get out of my sight.'

I had to go upstairs. I couldn't stand. My legs just wobbled. I edged step by step. My chest really hurt, my throat hurt, but I just had to get up the stairs before she came back. I got into bed. I was still finding it hard to breathe. Why, why, why did I go and ask to watch TV? Deep down, maybe, I didn't think she'd say no in front of my nan. I did learn my lesson. She was angry with me for ages after that. I was either sent to my room or sent to the little cupboard under the stairs where the hoover was kept. It was only a small cupboard and so I had to crawl in. It was dark and horrible in there. I was so scared, not only of spiders, but also whenever anyone went up or down the stairs it sounded so loud that I thought that the house was going to fall in on me.

One evening soon afterwards she got me from my bedroom and said we were going to have a little chat. The boys were in bed and there was no sign of my dad. Mum sat at the table with her tape recorder. I had to stand next to her.

'Why did you ask to watch telly after I told you not to?'

I was starting to get scared again. She said it in a calm voice but my stomach knew – it started trembling.

'I'm sorry.'

Smack.

'That's not an answer.'

I knew now that this wasn't going to be a nice chat. We did occasionally have them. At those times she would tell me that she loved me but I must try harder, and she would call me Susie.

'I thought you said that I wasn't allowed to watch *Top of the Pops*.' I'd only asked because I thought she might have changed her mind.

Smack.

'You knew damn well what I meant, didn't you?'

Smack.

I fell to the floor. When I stood up I tried to move an inch or two away. I don't know why I always edged away, for, if she missed, it made her even more angry and I would get it even worse. She now put her hands on my shoulders and steered me into the correct position. I hated standing there, knowing that a slap, a punch or a kick could hit me at any moment.

'Get here. I didn't have to take you in, you know.'

'Yes, Mum.'

'There are not many women who would have. Why are you always so bad?'

'I don't know.'

Smack.

'Why do you lie? Well?'

I didn't know what to say, so I whispered, 'I'm sorry.'

'Speak up and into the tape.'

I hadn't realised that I was being taped, though I'd heard Mum and the boys singing into the tape recorder and playing it back while I was washing up one night.

'Why do you go out of your way to shit-stir?'

'I don't mean to,' I whispered.

Smack.

'INTO THE TAPE! The boys don't give me trouble. Why do you?'

'I don't know.'

Smack.

Even though I hated my room, at this moment I wished I could be there. Crying was a waste of time, as she never seemed to see the tears. She carried on asking me questions and smacking me across the face while taping it. When the tape was finished I was allowed to go to bed.

The next few months were a very bad time. I was sent to bed a lot and I rarely saw my father. One day he went storming out of the house, so I was sent to bed. If nobody came to get me for tea, I knew I wasn't having any. Still, it was Monday tomorrow and I'd get my school dinner. Paul came up to tell me I had to do the dishes. After I'd washed them I was about to go back to bed when Mum appeared. I don't know what I'd done or said, but all of a sudden I was bent backwards over the kitchen table with the bread knife at my throat.

'I'll do it one day. I really will.' Her eyes were blazing, they were so full of hate. I tried to swallow but a huge lump had appeared in my throat. I really thought that I was going to die. I didn't bother pleading with her. I just closed my eyes and waited.

Someone came into the kitchen, I think it was Anthony, and he shouted, 'Mummy, what are doing?' It seemed to bring her to her senses and she let me go. I ran up to bed and cried my eyes out. What had I done to make her so angry? For the first time I thought that I was going to die. If she had killed me, she would have been sent to prison and it would all be my fault. I was starting to wish that my real mother would hurry up and come back and get me.

I tried to look forward to Christmas, especially as Margaret and her family were coming over on Christmas Eve. That evening all we children were in bed but we could hear them downstairs. It all sounded like great fun. Everyone seemed to be laughing. We got up at about 3am to open our presents. Mum opened one of hers and it was a nightdress from my dad. I had the exact same one but when she saw mine she gave me 'the look'. The rest of the day went OK. I went to bed and fell asleep but was awoken in the night when Mum came in. She took all my presents and threw them into a black bin bag. She didn't say a word. I would have rather had a beating than lose all my presents, but then I would eventually have lost them one by one anyway.

I lay awake for most of the night. Recently I had been doing that a lot as I was always trying to work things out in my mind; trying to figure out what was the best thing to do. My real mother was entering my thoughts again. Was she out there thinking about me? I was starting to wonder what she was like. I imagined her coming to take me away to live with her. We would go shopping or read together and she would teach me how to cook. We could do all the things that normal families did.

On Boxing Day Mum's sister came over with her kids, who were roughly the same age as us. One of my cousins came into my room and asked where my presents were. 'Downstairs,' I replied, praying he would change the subject. I couldn't say that Mum had thrown them away as then he would have known that I was really bad to have made her do a thing like that.

Mum said nothing about my presents. While washing up I was tempted to take a look in the dustbin, but I didn't. I didn't want to see them at the bottom of the bin. We all played outside in the evening. At teatime chocolate cake was offered around but I said, no, thank you. Mum had given me that look again, and it just wasn't worth it.

FOUR

The next big event was the birth of my little sister. I don't remember much about Karen when she was a baby apart from making her bottles of food. I would take six bottles out of the box, put eight scoops of powder in them, pour hot water into them until it reached number eight on the scale on the side and then wash the other six dirty ones with a funny-looking brush, dry them and put them back in the box.

One night Mum came into my room and started thumping me. As I was in bed I tried to slip under the blankets, but she pulled me out by my hair. She was then able to get to my throat and started to strangle me. I did once think about pretending to be dead. Would she stop then? I was a 'fucking bitch', a 'whore' and a 'shitface'. Every name came out of her mouth. There was a girl at school whose surname was Horwood and she was often teased about being a 'whore', but I didn't know what it meant. Sometimes Mum just completely baffled me with her name-calling. She once told me that I was a slapper, just like my mother was, but she was the one that was actually slapping me. I didn't understand.

'If you ever go near Karen again, I'll kill you.'

Apparently she had gone to make an extra bottle for Karen and had noticed that I hadn't cleaned it properly: there was a small milk mark on the neck. The necks were always tricky to clean, but she thought that I was trying to poison Karen. So I was never allowed to play with her. She was a beautiful baby, with blonde hair and big blue eyes. Everyone loved her.

I was now eight and started at middle school. I had a red jumper. I loved red. Our school uniforms were always immaculate. I walked to my school, which was just across the road from my first school. I wished Mum could have come with me as I noticed all the other kids had their mums with them and some had their dads too. The school was a Church of England school, although we weren't a particularly religious family. My brothers and I all went to the first school but the middle school only opened when Paul was due to start, so Anthony and Andrew were in different schools. As ours was a C of E school and it was the 1970s, we received a lot of bomb threats and often had to spend an afternoon in our church while the school was being checked.

'That's your people doing that,' my mum told me. I didn't have a clue what she meant. My people! Who were my people and why would they want to blow up my friends? I kept very quiet during bomb threats. I didn't want anyone else to find out.

I loved my school. My form teacher made up a game called

Fizz Buzz. We all stood in a long line and called out the numbers in sequence, starting from one. At multiples of three we would say, 'Fizz', at multiples of four we would say, 'Buzz' and at multiples of both we would say, 'Fizz buzz'. So it went, 'One, two, fizz, buzz, five, fizz, seven, buzz, fizz, ten, eleven, fizz buzz, thirteen' and so on. When you got it wrong you had to sit down. I loved that game. I practised at home in my bedroom, not just with threes and fours but with all numbers, so when the teacher changed them I would be ready.

I used to sit next to a girl called Sarah. I was as skinny as a stick and she was quite large. The rest of the class would call us Fatty and Skinny and make up rhymes about us. I loved being one of the popular ones. Sarah was a packed-lunch girl and I would look out for her arrival at school as she had food and would generously share it with me. Everyone knew me as I often cracked jokes or was cheeky to the teacher, but he used to make me stand on a chair and put my hands on my head.

'Who looks the fool now?' he would say.

I so wanted to say, 'You, sir', but didn't dare. If I got into too much trouble at school I would get sent to the headmaster, and I was so scared that my dad would find out.

I especially loved sports, but I'll always remember Monday mornings, when our first lesson was to write about 'What I did at the weekend'. Some kids would call out, 'We didn't do anything, sir.'

'You must have done something,' the teacher would say.

But most weekends I really didn't do anything. So I made up stories. It was easy: I just imagined what I could be doing with my real mother.

One day I woke up to get ready for school and found my shoes were gone. Mum was downstairs, which was unusual, as she was usually in bed in the morning. She was washing the clothes. For ten minutes I stayed upstairs trying to work out what to do. I knew I had to go down and tell her, but I just wanted to make sure there wasn't an alternative. There wasn't, so I went down. It was nearly eight o'clock, so I did my dusting and went to find my mum.

'I can't find my shoes,' I said.

She was now pulling out clothes from the washing part of the machine and putting it into the spinning part. To do this she used large wooden tongs, which I was very scared of.

'Well, you better find them,' she said.

I went away and looked in the shoe cupboard in the porch, but anyone could see that they weren't there. The boys left for school and through the glass front door I could see all the other kids from my road going to school. A feeling of despair swept over me and I just didn't know what to do. I wished I could open the door and scream to someone to help me or just tell me what I should do. I wanted to ignore my stomach, which was already starting to get knotty. I wanted to have the feeling that everything was going to be OK, but I knew it wouldn't be. No matter how much I wished for everything to be OK, it never was. I had to go back to her. I hoped we could sort it out quickly and then maybe I could still go to school. It was now 8.20.

'I'm sorry, Mum, but I can't find them.'

'Get here.'

Oh no! I had to stand within smacking distance. The washing machine was steaming and I was getting really scared.

'So, what are you going to do?' she asked.

'Could I wear my plimsolls?'

Slap.

'No.'

'Could I borrow one of the boys' pairs?'

'No.'

Slap.

This one was a hard one and made my head bang against the wall. I thought about it and came up with the perfect answer.

'Could I borrow one of your pairs?'

Smack.

I didn't see the hand coming this time and it knocked me over and she followed it with a kick. I now decided that I should try to move away a little after every slap. Sometimes I couldn't help myself. She would place me in my smacking spot but my body instinctively edged away. I knew that things would get worse if she missed, but it was a normal reaction. My brain was saying stay but my body was saying move.

'Get up. What are you going to wear to school?'

Eight thirty-five. It would take me ten minutes to walk to school, which started at 8.50. I had five minutes to find the answer.

'Well?'

'I don't know.'

Slap.

I knew I must never say that. But I really didn't know. There was no possible answer and I really wanted to go to school. Not only to get out of there but also because I hadn't had any breakfast. I wasn't allowed breakfast until my shoes were cleaned.

I really wanted the school dinner. Eight forty-five. I could run and still make it, but I knew I wasn't going to school today. I had a sneaky suspicion that Mum had hidden my shoes. But why would she do that? I had to stand there and watch her finish her washing.

'It's hard work, isn't it?' she said.

'Yes, Mum.'

'I suppose you think I sit around all day doing nothing.'

'No, Mum.'

'What do I do then?'

'I don't know.'

'I'll show you then.' With that she pulled my hair in a bunch and dragged me into every room, and there I had to tell her what she did in that room. If I forgot something she would twist me around, so her grip was tighter. We got to the sitting room and she said, 'The dusting?'

But I did the dusting every morning. I didn't dare say anything, though. We got to the bathroom with her still holding my hair.

'Clean the toilet, the bath, the sinks, wash the floor, wash the towels and clean the cabinet.' I couldn't have missed out anything, as it was only a small room. She banged my head in the sink and said, 'What about the taps?' It felt as if she had split my head open, but above the pain I remembered thinking that it wasn't fair as the taps were part of the sink. I was flung into my room. I could feel a bump appearing on the top of my head but luckily my fringe would hide it.

I didn't get to go on many school trips. As soon as I'd get a letter I would be on my best behaviour. I would dust the ornaments so hard they would sparkle. I would make sure that Karen's bottles were gleaming. I would do anything I could, but more often than not I wouldn't be allowed to go. I had come to the conclusion that I was a bad child and because of that I wasn't allowed nice treats.

After school was much the same. If no one was there other than my stepmother, I was most likely to be sent to bed. Or more precisely she would yell at me, 'Get out of my sight!' At least I had my Fizz Buzz to practise and I was also dreaming of my life with my real mum. My birthday had been and gone. I was always thinking about her on my birthday and always wondered if she was thinking of me. I had hoped that now I was eight I might get a birthday card from her. Maybe Mum was destroying them because she didn't like my real mother.

One day after school I was sent upstairs to get changed out of my uniform and into smart clothes. Mum came into my room and said, 'If anyone asks, then you were playing up the park with your brothers. And that's how you got them.'

'Yes, Mum.'

I didn't know who 'anyone' might be or what she meant by 'got them'. Got what? But I knew better than to dare to question her. I went downstairs and there was a ginger-haired lady sitting at the table drinking orange squash.

'Hello, Susan. How are you?'

'I'm very well, thank you.' I noticed white bits had appeared on the top of her orange squash. I wondered if she'd swish them away with her finger, the same way that we children did.

'My name is Kate. Your mum tells me you're getting on well at school. Do you enjoy it?'

33

'Yes, thank you.'

'What do you like the most?'

I wanted to say Fizz Buzz but was scared to in case Mum somehow stopped me from playing it.

'Maths,' I replied.

Mum told me to go to the garden and play. I wanted to ride my brother's bike, which was lying on the floor, or go on the swing, but I knew I'd get in trouble, so I played hopscotch instead.

The lady went and I was sent upstairs: not to go to bed but to change. I was allowed to stay downstairs for the evening. When we went to bed Anthony said that they had also been told to say that they were fighting with me at the park. And if they didn't say it I would be taken away into a home. He told me that the lady, Kate, was a social worker and went round looking for kids to put into her home.

'Why?' I asked him, but he didn't know.

I was scared. I didn't want to go to 'the home'. I lay and worried about this for a while but the words 'That's how you got them' kept entering my mind. I had very rarely been to the park with my brothers. It just didn't make sense, unless Mum was talking about my bruises. I always had loads of them on my body, but never on my face. There she would slap me, and once she punched me in the mouth and her ring cut me and I began to bleed. My dad was in at the time, so I had to have a towel on my face and pretend that I'd had a nosebleed.

But my body, especially my back, had loads of bruises on it. I didn't really take much notice of them as they never really hurt and they were always hidden under my clothes. Sometimes

I would check just to see what colour they had become. It fascinated me to see them go from bright purple to a dull yellow within a few days. I still didn't understand why this woman would want to come and take me away.

She came back a couple of times but just asked the same questions. When I was out in the street I knew when she was at our house because she parked her moped outside our front garden. I didn't like her. I thought she was nasty. My parents didn't like her either, and whenever she left they always talked about her, calling her an interfering busybody or a know-it-all.

One day my father was arrested. He'd been caught stealing from Sainsbury's. After that we were never allowed to go in there. I thought they had barred the whole family, but stopping us going there was my dad's way of protesting at them. He had spent loads of money on shopping, but they still had him arrested. He felt it was right to help himself to a bottle of rum after all the money he had spent there. So we always had to walk all the way to Tesco's. This didn't really affect me as I rarely went shopping, but I was glad he told us. I liked being told things that were happening as it made me feel important and like part of the family.

Karen was 20 months old now and running around all over the place. She loved *The Muppet Show* and had her own Kermit. Mum had a baby boy, Steven, in March 1979. Again I didn't see much of him as a baby. I had to do the bottles, which were inspected daily to see if I had done them correctly.

One Sunday afternoon I was allowed to take Karen up to the local park. 'Be careful with her and I'll be checking on her for any pinches or smacks,' Mum said. Why would I want to hurt Karen? She was such a lovely baby. I pushed her, in her buggy, up the hill. We had fun. I pushed her on the baby swings, sat with her on the roundabout and went down the slide with her. I was her big sister.

Unfortunately, Karen kicked up a right fuss when she had to leave the park. We had to get home for Sunday dinner, but every time I tried to pick her up she started screaming. A lady saw me and I was so scared she would tell Mum that I was hurting Karen. I didn't know what to do. I was so lucky that Paul appeared. Dinner was ready and he'd come to tell us. He picked Karen up and I pushed the empty buggy. She didn't scream as much now as she was obviously used to Paul. I still enjoyed the morning and thought that after a while she would also get used to me and wouldn't cry or scream any more.

Things were starting to improve slightly. I now shared a room with Karen, which meant that my dad's 'sex stuff' became non-existent and my mum's night-time beatings also stopped. I slept on the top bunk, which, fortunately for me, meant I was harder to get to. I was also allowed to stay up more in the evenings and go out more. Steven was one, Karen was now nearly three, Paul was due to start high school and I would soon be in the top form of middle school. It was a good summer and in the evenings Andy Evans, Margaret's 18-year-old son, would come over. He would take me to the off-licence to buy my brothers and me a big bag of crisps each.

In September I started in the fourth form at school. A couple of weeks later Mum took me into the shed for a private chat.

'I'm leaving on Friday and I need you to help me get my stuff out,' she said.

Why was she leaving? What had I done? And why was she being nice and telling me?

'You can't tell anyone but I am going away with Andy and having his baby.'

'Yes, Mum.'

And that was it.

The only person that I told was my PE teacher and I only told her because she wanted to put me in the netball team. I said I wouldn't be able to play because I would probably be needed at home to help look after the babies.

The following Friday I went to school as normal and rushed home like Mum had told me to. I waited outside with her shopping basket. We went out and we walked around the corner to the Johnsons' house. I just sat on the chair. Andy turned up on his motorbike. How are they going to get the shopping basket on that? I thought to myself. Andy stayed for a cup of tea and then asked Mum if she was ready.

'Look after Karen,' Mum said. 'Goodbye.'

And then she went. I couldn't stop crying. I had never cried in front of the Johnsons but I couldn't help it.

'What are you crying for?' Dave asked.

'Dad, her mum just left!' said his son.

Dave looked at me. 'This is the best thing that's ever happened to you!'

I went home pulling my now empty basket. I had to give Dad a note and afterwards I went up to my room and cried.

FIVE

Over the next few months my life completely turned around. I got a weekend job helping a milkman, and with the money I would go swimming and buy records and sweets. I could play football with the boys at school. I could play with Kim. Mum had fallen out with Kim's mum years before and I'd been forbidden to go anywhere near my friend. Now I could do what I wanted, when I wanted and with whoever I wanted. Nobody was ever going to tell me what to do again.

Karen was three and Steven was 18 months when Mum left, and so for the next six months my auntie, then my nan and then my granddad looked after them, before finally they were placed in temporary foster care. Sunday night to Friday night they lived with a family in Northolt. Kate, the orange squash-drinking moped rider, was back on the scene, ready to take my little brother and sister, or so Deidre had led me to believe.

My three older brothers were now entering their teens and

there was a lot of arguing and fighting going on. One by one locks started appearing on the doors. For me it was handy if I wanted to keep out an annoying brother, but it didn't prevent a perverted father from coming in. He insisted on having a spare key, 'in case there's a fire'. My dad's interest in my body was, due to my sudden development, becoming more intense. I hated my body. I wanted to be one of the boys, ride my bike, play football, fight. I didn't want to be a girl. But I was and had to put up with my dad watching me dress or bath, for he always managed to turn up whenever I was about to jump into the tub. I was really uncomfortable with him leering all over me while his hand was working away inside his trousers.

I was very embarrassed about my body and just wanted to keep it under wraps. Kim's mum and dad both went out to work, so she would let me shower at her house. I would use the excuse that, coming from a big family, I could never get into the bathroom. I was very good at lying. Unfortunately, my body continued to develop and my dad was not content with just looking; he wanted more. At first, after these incidents, he would buy me gifts, pay for a school trip to France – all the nice things I had previously longed for I was now getting.

Dave still came round with his two boys. His youngest was nearly my age and we were friends. My dad had converted the downstairs living room into his bedroom-cum-bar and he and Dave used to sit up at the bar listening to music, smoking and drinking and having a good laugh. It all sounded so merry.

After they had gone my dad would give me cigarettes and drinks and I willingly took them. I thought it made me look tough and grown up. They came with a price, though. I liked the good things I was getting, but I didn't like what I had to do to get them. But gradually I learned how to speed up the process and sometimes I would be lucky and manage to avoid it completely. I would pretend to hear one of the younger ones crying, or one of my older brothers' footsteps. When my dad went to the bathroom I would quickly turn everything off so that when he came back he would just think, in his drunken state, that he had been getting ready for bed. He'd call out for me, but I would be hiding in the larder. He'd go to bed then, probably a bit confused. Or I would pretend to feel sick and would go up to bed, but I had to stop using this excuse, because once he came up a few minutes later and, calling out loudly because he was sozzled, he wanted to know why I wasn't downstairs. I quickly went down. I didn't want Karen and Steven or my older brothers knowing what I was doing.

I was really beginning to hate it. And to hate myself for doing it. Before, when I was younger, my dad's 'sex stuff' had been very quick and he was sober. But now he was drunk each time, which meant that he was sweaty and smelly, and I really hated this dirty man all over me. And it always took ages and ages for it to be all over.

There were times when I would be lying in bed, trying desperately to sleep, but could hear my dad crashing about downstairs. I knew the sound that I would hear next would be him outside my bedroom door, fumbling with his keys, trying to find the right one for my lock. Or I'd hear a loud thump downstairs and knew that he had fallen over. Then I would lie there in total turmoil. I didn't want to go down and check to see if he was OK in case he was and wanted me for the 'sex stuff' again What if he really had fallen over and hurt himself and was lying there unconscious, perhaps even dying? I'd lie there praying that I'd hear some sort of noise so that I'd know that he was up and about again. As I lay there waiting to hear something I'd have visions of him lying on the floor bleeding to death. I had no choice but to go downstairs.

My dad went to the pub every Monday night, and one night Anthony knocked at my door and told me to watch the telly. There was a little boy floating at the window, telling his brother to let him in. Then he opened his mouth, which revealed that he was actually a vampire. I was so scared. Dad came home drunk and couldn't find the back-door key, so he woke my older brothers and me and kicked us out into the back garden and locked us out. We had to stay there until the key was found. As it was eleven o'clock and we were all in our nightwear, there wasn't much chance of the missing key being found. All I could do was watch the sky just in case little boys were floating around. I kept very close to Anthony. I was so scared.

Paul managed to climb through the bathroom window and let us in. I felt very relieved once I got back into bed that night, although I felt very hurt that my dad could do such a thing to me. I also felt scared of vampires and so I turned away from the window. You would never know one until it was too late. Isn't it funny that people can seem so normal one minute and then turn into evil monsters the next?

I was looking forward to Christmas again this year. I had loads of presents for Karen and Steven. My older brothers also had jobs and so the younger two kids were going to be really spoiled. They seemed so lost, not really knowing what was going on. On Christmas Day my dad woke me at 3.30 so that I could go and do my milk round. (He never allowed us a day off.) When I got back we opened our presents. It was a good day. I was starting to relax a little more now, but I was still terrified that my stepmother would come back, because she still occasionally turned up to see Karen. She had sent everyone apart from me a Christmas card. I was a little hurt by this as I thought we were friends now that I had helped her get away. I just told myself that the postman must have lost it. He did have quite a big bag. I had also heard my dad talking to her on the phone, pleading with her to come back home. She rang once and I answered the phone.

'Is your father there?' she asked.

'No,' I replied.

'Where is he then?'

'I don't know.' Whoops, I forgot. I was never allowed to say that as she hated it.

'Well, what time will he be home?'

'How would I know?' I was feeling really brave after my 'I don't know'.

'You just remember who you're talking to,' she said.

My stomach started to tremble. I was still scared of her.

She soon stopped coming to our house to visit Karen. Everyone, apart from me, was very hostile towards her. I felt very sorry for little Steven, as it was only ever Karen that she spent her time with. She showed little interest in him. I knew how hard it was to accept the fact that your mother didn't want you. But I was 11 and he was only two.

Generally, I was enjoying my life and my newfound freedom. She was gone and nobody was ever going to tell me what to do again, which caused many problems at school. Now I was from a broken family and I had been instantly labelled a 'problem child'. I was getting into all sorts of trouble. The headmaster would write to my dad, who would molest me and then forgive me, and I would go back to school even more moody, bad-tempered and full of self-hate. Then I would get into trouble again and the whole cycle would repeat itself. I did still feel immensely guilty about everything and even more sorry for my dad. First his mum dying and now his wife gone. Most Saturday mornings I would get up at five to start my milk round and he would be slumped drunkenly over the dining table, his sad songs playing in the background.

The biggest highlight of my life at the time was that I was now allowed to play in the school sports teams. I really enjoyed playing netball and would get all excited when a match was arranged. One time I couldn't play very well as my dad had been abusing me the night before and had made me very sore. We had to wear small PE skirts and I was too scared to jump about in case anyone saw. I would have died of embarrassment and shame.

I was soon to start high school, and I was looking forward to it very much. I worked all summer to pay for my uniform. We got a school grant, but only every other year, and it wasn't due until the following summer. I was determined to be the model student. I was going to be in all the sports teams, all the top sets in class. I was going to be the best. And soon I was in the top sets and all the sports teams, but, because of my problem with accepting orders, things didn't turn out quite according to plan. I couldn't stand the way some teachers tried to belittle me in front of the whole class, so I gave them hell.

I carried on enjoying sports at high school and now I had been introduced to hockey, which I absolutely loved. There was never a day when I was home at the normal time as I was either playing in a match or practising. My PE teacher was brilliant. Not only would she compliment me and encourage me to push myself further, but she would also stick up for me when I was in trouble with other teachers. I liked her. She was probably the first person I really did like.

SIX

Not long after I started high school my dad was caught drink-driving and lost his licence and with it his job. Kate, the social worker, immediately appeared. Because of what my mum had said about her, I felt sure she wanted Karen and Steven for her home, but as my dad could no longer work he became a stay-at-home father looking after them. I was growing to love the two little ones very much and was very protective towards them. Sometimes I felt very guilty for driving their mother away – like I had my own, as I saw it – and wanted to make it up to them.

With Dad now out of work we all of a sudden became very poor. Dave still came round for drinks. More than once I had to run around to the off-licence to get a bottle of whisky, as Dad just couldn't say, 'No, sorry, I don't have any.' We ate shepherd's pie made with baked beans and porridge oats instead of meat, but Dave still got a drink.

Karen was due to start school, so I worked all summer again

to pay for her uniform. She looked so lovely in it. I took her to school and it was mainly me who picked her up. One morning it was snowing hard, so I carried her all the way to school only to find that it was closed, and I had to carry her all the way back. When Steven started I took him as well. I had to give up most of my sports as my school day ended at 3pm and I had to be at the kids' school at 3.30.

I was starting to get very tired and I was nearly always late for school, but if the teachers ever said anything I would just give them a mouthful. My dad had got my older brothers and me paper rounds, which we had to do every Friday evening. In the holidays he got us a leaflet round and we had to deliver leaflets to a thousand houses each day – and that was after doing our milk rounds. But I still managed to have some fun. Kim and I were proper little tomboys. We would swing on ropes over the river, climb on rooftops and jump from one to another – if we'd missed we would have broken our necks – and there was a green-tiled roof we used to slide down, though we had to stop that because it stained our jeans. Or we'd start at the top of the hill and run through all the gardens, climbing or leaping over walls and fences until we reached the bottom. Once we found an old underground air-raid shelter and managed to prise the top off so we could jump down inside and explore. In the car park we would sit on bread trays and slide down the slopes. Some days we would ride our bikes for miles down the canal, stopping only for ciggie breaks.

I didn't really have anything to do with my older brothers. Anthony was very quiet and was always in his room, which he shared with Steven. Andrew was a right hard nut. He slept in the loft. Paul was just a bit too snidey. He lived out in the shed, as he and my dad didn't get along at all. Andrew was always my dad's favourite and I think Paul was a bit envious of this. But, to be honest, my dad never really took much notice of anything any of us did. When I told him I was in the top sets at school he never said, 'Well done' or, 'I'm so proud'; he would just grunt and give his 'so what?' look.

To him everything was work and money – that was the priority – but it didn't benefit the family. I felt it went instead to his friends. My friends, my brothers and I would be charged 35p for a can of drink, but not the others: they could have whatever they wanted and not pay a penny. My dad was quite kind to us, though, and if we couldn't afford to pay he made a note in his little book and we could pay him later.

For my holidays I went on the coach to my granddad, who lived on the Isle of Wight. I had to pay for my coach ticket, but Dad would pay for Karen and Steven's. I loved it at my granddad's. Not only was I away from my abusive father, but also we got to eat nice food. My granddad's wife, Auntie Hilary, was my dad's stepmother. She was a lovely lady who would do anything for us. She cooked us a breakfast every day. It was the only time I ever ate sausages as they were never on the dinner menu at school and we didn't get them at home. I never saw Auntie Hilary angry or even raise her voice to anyone. I felt so safe there. She would always tell me how great my dad was and how I should always remember that. She didn't need to tell me that. I knew it already.

Kim, an only child, was my best friend, though most of the time we were sworn enemies. We had the same taste in music and we were always swapping tapes. One night we were playing Monopoly at her house when she put on a tape. It was the one Mum had made that night when she was questioning me. I told Kim to turn it off, as I didn't want to be reminded. After that we went on playing very quietly.

She wanted me to go on holiday with her to Jersey, but I couldn't afford it. A few days later she rang me (even though we lived only nine houses apart) to tell me that her dad had got me a job tidying up an American man's house. He, John, had moved into number 42 (Kim lived at 50 and I at 68) and was a messy guy, so he needed someone to tidy up for him once a week and was offering £5.

John was due to stay in England for the next three years, working for the American Embassy, after being in posts in different parts of the world. Kim and I decided we'd like to share the job. Her dad was friendly with John and so she was given the OK. I asked my dad, who said yes as soon as the £5 was mentioned, even though he had never met the guy. John, who drove a big, flash American camper van, also impressed us with the goodies from the States he gave us. At school we would show off the sweets, bubblegum and cans of soft drink with their funny ring-pulls.

As time went by I gradually started to really like the man. We went shopping in London together and he took me all over the country, visiting places, canoeing sometimes, and we had loads of fun. He would even come and watch me play hockey. My parents had never come to the school to see me do anything; they hadn't even attended any of the open evenings. But then it became obvious that he fancied me.

When his younger brother came over for a visit with his wife and three young daughters, John clearly doted on the girls. When the family left he was heartbroken and I wanted to make him feel better. We ended up in bed but we didn't have sex: he just lay in my arms. From that moment on I felt sure that I was in love with John.

I didn't really have any boyfriends. There was one boy who, when he came round with his dad Dave, used to knock at my bedroom door and we would mess around, but the next day he would pretend he didn't know me. Another boy, Terry, used to treat me like shit in front of other people, but when no one else was around he would tell me he loved me. I believed him. 'Do this,' he would say, and I did, even though I hated it. I just thought that was what boyfriends and girlfriends did. And John would have liked sex and now I was beginning to want him too, but I just couldn't do it and kept on rejecting him.

I didn't push my dad off, though. He was still abusing me quite often, but by now I'd realised that if I'd had a few vodkas it didn't seem so bad. I could be somewhere else: my body was there but it was an empty shell. When my mum used to hit me, I managed to cut off from the pain my body was receiving, though my mind was more alert. But with him I wasn't there in body or mind.

By this time I was often getting into serious trouble at school. I had dropped down to the middle sets and been suspended many times. One of my teachers used to tell me to not bother coming to his lessons any more, so I did what he said. I really didn't care. My favourite teacher had left, so now I never bothered about PE either. I did join a women's football team, though, and played a couple of matches for them, but I was always very embarrassed about changing in front of them, so I had to quit.

John saw how bad things were and tried to help. He arranged for me to go and live with his parents in the States and even managed to get me a place in a local school. But there were problems: it turned out that I didn't have a legal guardian. My dad and stepmother never adopted me and my natural mother had just disappeared, so I didn't really belong to anyone. I was a bit upset that I wasn't a proper Hamford, for after all he was my real dad and I hated being the odd one out. John and the deputy head of my school managed to get it sorted. I didn't know how they'd done it, but I was very curious to know if they'd made contact with my natural mum. As I was the kid who didn't give a damn about anything, I couldn't ask.

When the new school year started and I went into the fifth form, everyone was nervous about exams, but I didn't care: I was due to go to America in January. Four more months and I would be off. Some of the other kids were envious of me, which secretly I felt pleased about. My dad didn't really say much and that hurt me a little. One night he came into my room for his normal 'sex stuff' after I'd had a few vodkas and I screamed at the top of my voice at him to get out. He did just that. It was that easy.

My leaving date was 10 January. My brothers weren't too bothered, the little ones were really too young to know I would be gone for good and my dad never said much about anything. He liked John for the cheap drinks he would get him but I think he blamed him for my putting a stop to the sex. Anyway,

I was ecstatic about going, but then a horrible, niggly thought kept entering my mind. Since I had yelled at my dad he had never come back. Was that because he knew I was going away and that little Karen would be in the room alone? I couldn't imagine him doing things like that with her, but then I realised I was even younger when he started on me. As much as I tried to find all the right reasons for going, there was still this one big reason not to go. I told John I couldn't do it. He was upset and said if I didn't pull myself together I was going to end up in the gutter. After that we never spoke again.

I carried on going into school but as they had thought I was leaving in January, I hadn't done my 'mocks' in the autumn term. That meant I wouldn't be entered for the CSE or O Level exams. The headmaster told me to go home and never come back. So I did. All of a sudden my bright and happy future was gone. But to me it was no great loss, for I didn't really have any hopes and dreams. All I wanted to do was grow up and get out. I suddenly realised that I'd just spent 11 years of my life at school and had nothing to show for it. John saying 'You'll end up in the gutter' really made me determined. I'll show him, I told myself, and I enrolled at a college in Hammersmith.

They wouldn't allow me to take O Levels straight away as I had missed so much of my last year at school, and I had to do a City and Guilds course for the first year. I started the course, but just getting to the college each day drained all my money. I was earning £5 for working Saturday and paying £5.50 for my travel card and I got no help towards it as the college wasn't in my local borough of Ealing. I took on extra paper rounds in the evening and managed to get by. I didn't enjoy college. It took me two hours to get there and two hours to get back. And as well as being totally skint all the time I owed my dad loads of money, thanks to his little IOU book.

But I got my O Levels and I was proud at my achievement, though no one else in the family made much of it. I think the best thing I got out of college was to meet one of my best mates, Wendy.

During my two years at college I was very mixed up. I was also very drunk most of the time. I couldn't afford to pay for the drinks and so my dad had to keep on getting out his little book. Around this time I was starting to ask myself questions. Why had Mum taken it out on me? Was it because I wasn't her daughter? But then, I thought, she had a daughter and just left her. Things were beginning to really bug me. I was expecting a card from my real mother on my eighteenth birthday. In fact I'd been half-expecting one every year. I'd go to bed the night before and practise how I would react if I did get one. But this year I would become an adult. Surely I would get one now. No card came. My birthdays were not happy days as I was always thinking about her and wondering if she was thinking about me.

Mother's Day was also a very depressing day. I had repeatedly asked my dad about my real mother. The story was that she was a young Catholic girl who had already had one daughter, who was being raised by a grandmother, so she couldn't possibly take me in. Besides, you were my baby. I wanted to have you,' my dad would say. It was in Devon, where he was a policeman, that he had met my mother. I pictured her as a poor country girl impressed with the uniform and powerful job that went with it. And I pictured her missing me, not really wanting to give me up, but having no choice in the matter.

I decided I would track her down. I contacted the Salvation Army and filled in the forms they sent, but the only information I had on her was her name and address at the time I was born, and they couldn't help me. They needed at least her date of birth. My dad didn't know precisely how old she was, and so that was that.

SEVEN

As my birthday is in July my dad discovered that he could continue to claim benefits for me for another whole year as long as I was in part-time education. So I enrolled in a number of evening classes, studying Law, Modern History, Geography and Child Psychology. I had to drop Child Psychology after we did a lesson about Sigmund Freud, who had stated that daughters actually wanted their fathers sexually, and I couldn't handle that. Besides it wasn't true. I didn't do anything to lead my dad on. How could I? I was only four years old when the 'sex stuff' first started. Was it my fault? I'd always tried to bury all memories of my dad's abuse. Anyway, all that had stopped. I did enjoy studying for the other subjects and as most of them were at local schools I wasn't spending all my pay on bus fares.

My dad also had a friend called Jack, who was married to a Polish lady named Rita. The couple would come round, quite frequently, for a drink at my dad's bar. One night Rita told off Karen, who ran upstairs crying. I looked at my dad, half expecting him to do something, but he didn't say or do anything.

I shot upstairs to comfort Karen and, from that moment on, I took an instant dislike to Rita. That autumn Rita introduced her Polish friend Ela to my dad. Due to my intense dislike towards Rita, I decided that I certainly was not going to like any friend of hers. My dad and Ela were fast becoming a couple and Ela moved in.

Anthony was in rented accommodation, Andrew was living with Mary (an old school friend of mine) and Paul had been kicked out of the house as my dad didn't like him, so we didn't know what was happening to him. I had been dating Mary's brother, who was also called Andrew, but when things started to get serious I dumped him. He was my first adult boyfriend, I think, but it felt like I was betraying my father. It was weird that throughout my childhood years I would do 'things' for boys, but now I had come to the age where it was OK to do these things, I just didn't want to. I was sick and tired of sex. If I never had to do it again I would be a happy person, I decided.

As I was now at home more, I could take care of Karen and Steven. I never missed any of their open evenings, sports days, the class assemblies held once a term or any other school activity to which a parental figure was invited. They were more to me than a brother and a sister. Yet now that it was just me and the little ones at home I felt extremely used. I was angry, hurt and felt worthless. My dad was happy that this woman would be 'Mum' to his two kids and they totally loved the idea of having a new mum. I couldn't blame them, as I would have loved to have a mum myself. I would have loved to have someone there that I could trust and ask all my growing-up questions. A mum could teach me how to be a proper lady.

About that time another bombshell dropped. I had washed my hair and while combing it back I noticed a small scar at the top of my ear. I pulled my ear forward and saw that the scar went nearly all the way down it. All at once my brothers' 'Van Gogh' and 'Vincent' taunts sprang into my mind. I had heard talk about my ear being torn off but didn't really think it was true. Now I knew it was. My mum had almost pulled my ear off. I was numb. All of a sudden I had flashbacks of Margaret Evans and the Johnsons teaching me how to speak. Was that why? Was I partially deaf? More importantly, how can someone have their ear hanging off and no one else does anything about it? What did the hospital say? Did my mum blame it on my brothers? For Christ's sake – a child with an ear half-hanging off! That's not a childhood accident! Why didn't anybody else in the family notice it? Surely my dad must have seen it.

Once again I felt very worthless and also very angry with everyone. Up until then I had always felt in a way lucky to be alive, for, after all, I should never have been born and also I'd escaped serious harm many times at Mum's hands. So I felt that every day was a bonus.

What made matters worse was that I had always believed my dad loved me, but with the arrival of Ela I started to wonder if he really did. I was falling deeper and deeper into depression. I was smoking heavily and drinking myself senseless. I didn't care.

One of my best friends at this time was Claudette, who had been in my class in high school. She was a quiet girl and, even though most of my schoolmates were very loud, we became friends. As I had been so down recently Claudette would come round to spend the evening with me, to try to cheer me up. Typically, I'd get drunk and we'd chat away into the night. We'd end up talking about our parents, as Claudette's dad was sometimes stern with his children.

'Well, at least your mum was OK,' I said to her one day.

'And you – at least your dad's OK,' she replied.

'No, my dad isn't. There's a lot of things he's done that you don't know about.'

At the time it seemed like a good idea to let it slip out. I wasn't totally drunk, but, if Claudette didn't believe me, I could say I'd made it up and blame it on the booze.

'Does he hit you?' she asked.

'No. It's worse than that.' That was all I said. Time to change the subject. But then I did get very drunk and managed to fall out of the loft, which was now my bedroom, and go crashing into my dad and Ela's room.

'Morning,' I said and picked myself up and staggered out.

The one good thing that I lived for was making sure that Karen and Steven were OK. I was determined to always be there for them. Unfortunately, with Ela's continued presence, they were slipping away from me. I felt that the best thing to do was to get away, so I applied to join the Army. It wasn't something that I really wanted to do – me taking orders! – but it was an escape route. I passed all the tests and exams and was about to go and sign on the dotted line, when I backed out. I couldn't leave the kids. What if Dad and Ela's relationship fell apart and she left? Karen and Steven would have lost another mum and then there would be nobody there for them. Even though I felt so trapped and hated seeing Ela taking over my role, I just couldn't do it.

A few days later a fierce argument occurred. I discovered that there had been an event at the kids' school which nobody had told me about. Dad and Ela had gone without me. When I found out I went crazy, and Ela and I got into a massive row and were shouting and screaming at each other. My dad told me to fuck off. I couldn't believe it. He had taken her side again. So I told him I was going to be using my original name, Jennifer Doonie, as I didn't want to be a Hamford any more. '"Father unknown," it says on my birth certificate,' I screamed at him, 'and you certainly have become very unknown.' And with that I stomped off to my bedroom.

Once again I felt very angry, hurt and worthless. Karen and Steven must have loved having two parents there. I know I would have done. But was I getting in the way and ruining everybody's happiness? I didn't know. I dwelled on it all night and became more and more upset. I didn't have anyone to talk to because, one by one, I had driven all my friends away. I don't need anyone, I had told myself, but I did: I had never felt so alone in my entire life. There was only one way out, I decided. I went into the kitchen and got loads of tablets – I don't even remember what they were now – and I washed the lot down with a bottle of bleach.

Half-choking, I staggered into my dad's bar and screamed, 'Now can you see that I'm hurting?'

He called an ambulance and gave me a glass of milk, which I threw on the floor. I wanted to tell him how hurt I'd been, but now I couldn't speak. The ambulance men came and took me to the hospital. I was starting to feel immensely embarrassed, as I didn't mean to cause all this trouble. I just wanted my dad to see how much I was hurting because then maybe he might do something about it. At the hospital I told them that my real name was Jennifer and was put into a ward with 'the other ones'. I shouldn't have been there: I wasn't crazy. While we were waiting for a bed my dad told me that I had hurt him with my 'father unknown' outburst. He left me a couple of quid, which I later discovered he had put down in his IOU book. He would come and pick me up tomorrow, he said.

It was the shittiest night of my life. I felt so stupid for being in hospital and wasting the nurses' valuable time. I felt guilty about hurting my dad and I hated myself more than ever. Nothing was ever mentioned about that night. I apologised to Ela and we eventually became friends. She was a diamond. She backed off a little with Karen and Steven and I kept myself to myself. I still wanted my real mum, though, and started thinking again that she would take me away and make everything all right. I checked the phone books in the local library, as I'd done several times before, just to see if she was now listed. While going through the pages my hands would always tremble. What would I do if I found her? But then I told myself, I'll worry about that if and when it happens. Her name wasn't listed. Devon was such a small place. I was so sure she would appear one day.

Both Kim and Claudette knew how I felt, and they rallied round, trying to cheer me up. Kim even said I could move in with her, but I still felt I couldn't leave the kids. Claudette and I were talking one night about possible jobs, when she mentioned that she had seen an advert for work with Royal Mail. I don't know why but I had made up my mind that I was going to be a prison warder, but I had to wait until I was 21 before I could apply, so I phoned about the Royal Mail job. Before long I'd passed the interviews and tests and was due to start at their training school at the end of September. I felt proud that one of the country's oldest and top employers had wanted me.

My brother Paul got married the weekend before I was due to start my training. It was purely by chance that we found him again after Dad kicked him out. Kim had been shopping and had noticed Paul working behind a counter. When she told me I immediately went to the shop and spoke to him. His girlfriend had given birth to a boy six months earlier. I was an auntie and I didn't know it.

The down side was that Paul's girlfriend was half-Indian and my dad hated all foreigners. Even though his new wife was Polish, she was OK as she was white. He had been arrested a few years back for being abusive and threatening to an Asian family who had moved in a few doors from us. His behaviour was so bad that they sold up and moved out. Another result was that afterwards we were never allowed to speak to Mr and Mrs Smith. They had been our neighbours two doors down and I always remember them throwing their vegetable waste over our gate so that we could feed it to our rabbits. Mr Smith had stood up to my dad and told him that his Indian neighbours were decent people and he should leave them alone. For this he was labelled a 'Paki-lover' and we weren't allowed to speak to the couple, which was a pity as I liked them; they were kind people.

My dad saw it as his duty to save England from being taken over! But now he and Ela were married and she was very keen on getting to know the family, so he accepted Paul and his quarter-Indian first grandchild.

Paul's wedding brought my first stepmother's mum to stay with us for a few days. She went on about how her daughter hadn't had to take me in, how much she loved me, how good and how proud of me she was and so on. I had to sit and listen to it all. I really didn't need it, and I got very drunk at Paul's wedding. Walking home, I apparently ran off from the rest of the family. I don't remember a thing about it. God knows where I went, but I woke the next day with my face, arms and legs grazed and cut. I was a total mess. I was due to start my Royal Mail training the next day. I rang Claudette, who gave me the number for Alcoholics Anonymous. That very day I was invited to a meeting but I never went again. I wasn't going to admit to being an alcoholic at 19.

When I arrived for my training I made up the story that I'd been pushing a broken-down car and it had suddenly jerked into life, knocking me flat on my face. After two weeks' training I was sent to work in my local post office in Greenford. It was a small office but it was full of all sorts of characters: scatty ones, ones with fags hanging out of their mouths, serious ones, grumpy ones, 'that's not on my contract – I'm not doing that' ones. I loved it. After Christmas I applied to become a driver and was sent on a two-week driving course. I passed and was very proud of my achievement. My dad didn't raise an eyebrow. I bought myself a car and could now go anywhere I wanted. That gave me a boost too. I was, however, getting fed up with being described as 'known as Susan Hamford' because legally I was still Jennifer. So I popped into the solicitor's office and changed my name by deed poll. I was now legally a Hamford. Again, my dad said nothing.

My twentieth birthday was fast approaching and I decided to have a small bash. I could never go out anywhere socially as I was very self-conscious, so I invited a few people from work, plus Wendy and her new husband, Kevin, to my house for a few drinks. It went OK. I didn't get too drunk and make a total prat of myself. I had some time off work to look forward to and the next day I was off to see my granddad on the Isle of Wight, where I bought some prezzies for the guys at work. Back at home after my visit, I awoke very early and found loads of ants crawling over my bedroom floor. I hate creepy-crawlies and so I had to get up. I thought I might as well drive in to work and give everyone their present.

Charlie and Carey rode in together, then Jenny appeared on her moped and then Darren drove in. I got chatting to Darren, who asked what I was going to be doing that day. I told him I would probably go for a spin, which I did. I ended up in Brighton. I'd just seen a sign and followed it. There I sat gazing out to sea. It was so sparkling blue on top yet so wild underneath. I always imagined a fish's life as being so peaceful, just swimming around all day. But it's not. The poor little thing has to be alert at all times, or else he's someone else's dinner. I suppose every living thing has to fight to survive. Maybe I shouldn't make a big deal about what has happened and just forget about it. But looking at the calm sea that summer's day just got me thinking. I had always believed that, no matter how bad things were for me, there was always someone worse off. Always. I just had to get over it. I had to forget about things and carry on with my life, but there were still so many unanswered questions.

I returned to work and bumped into Darren. We got chatting and I told him I might go to Brighton again at the weekend. I decided that he was an OK guy. On Saturday I finished at 10.15 and went out to look for him. After a lot of umming and aahing I asked him if he wanted to come with me. Yes, he said. So on the Sunday we had our first date. I called at Darren's house at about 6am to discover that his dad had just made him a lovely breakfast. On a Sunday, he told me, his dad always cooked a hot breakfast for him and the rest of the family. I was a little taken aback by this. What a nice dad he had!

EIGHT

By Christmas Darren had moved in with me at my dad's. By Easter I was pregnant. I couldn't believe it. It was so unfair. I didn't even like sex! I would use every possible excuse to get out of doing it. I would have the longest periods ever or we couldn't do it as I was due 'on' any time now. I'd have a headache or something else wrong just to get out of it. How could I have let this happen?

I knew why. During all sexual activity I had either switched off or had been drunk. Being drunk allowed me to do anything, and if my actions were wrong I could just blame it on the booze. I now wished that I'd been to the family planning clinic. I had been once before, during my teens, after my doctor recommended that I go on the pill because I had been experiencing irregular periods. I went along to the clinic but had to leave because I felt so embarrassed. I wanted everyone to know that I wasn't there because I was planning on having sex, but for other reasons. I should have gone back but

I knew that I would never be able to sit among all the other women. I'd imagine everyone looking at me thinking, Yep, I know what she's going to be doing. The slut!

That day I did three pregnancy tests and they were all positive, but I didn't believe them. I had bought the kits from a small chemist's, the only one I could find open on a Sunday. They were probably out of date. I'll get one from Boots tomorrow, I decided, and then I'll definitely know. I did and that one was also positive.

We then had to move out of my dad's as he said we'd never get a council flat if we still lived at home. On Thursday, 13 July we were sitting in the council's housing department – what a depressing place! Two days later it would be my twenty-first birthday and I still hoped that Mum would remember me and send me a card. But she didn't. The family had lived in the same house all my life and we had such an unusual name that I felt certain she could have easily contacted me if she'd wanted to. That's definitely it now, I said to myself, I'll have to forget about her and concentrate on my new family.

My pregnancy went very smoothly. I was never sick and I never had any unusual cravings, which was a pity, as I was looking forward to sending Darren out in the middle of the night to get me something weird and wonderful. I was very energetic and kept losing weight, which the doctors were very concerned about, warning me that they would admit me to hospital unless I calmed down. I did calm down, but then the thought of going into hospital began to scare me. I had to register with my doctor as it was discovered that, even though I had been going to the same one all my life, I wasn't actually a patient of his because my parents had never registered me. It didn't really surprise me. In fact, it answered the question of how my mum got away with causing my injuries.

I still felt nervous with medical people, but I guess most people do. I was always immensely embarrassed whenever the nurses asked about family illnesses. I never liked anyone knowing the fact that my mother just left me, as it's not a thing mothers tend to do, so I just said there was nothing.

During one check-up I was asked to give a blood sample. While I stretched out my arm, the nurse asked, 'When did you break it?' I didn't know what to say. I had heard rumours of Mum breaking my arm but didn't think any more about it. If she had broken my arm, that would have meant hospital treatment and surely questions would have been asked. Maybe they were asked but, if they never registered me with the doctor, perhaps they gave a false name at the hospital – maybe they used my real name, Jennifer.

I went to my dad's and asked him about my arm. 'Yes,' he said, 'your mum pulled you out of your cot and it just snapped.'

A little angry flame started flaring up inside me, but I had to just push it away and try to forget it. I kept telling myself that it didn't matter any more – it was over.

Back at home – the council had given us a temporary flat right next to Karen's school and she would often drop in and stay over – my due date, 20 December, was fast approaching. I could feel my baby kicking and had seen it on the scan, but I still couldn't believe that I was going to have a baby. The due date came and went. On Friday, 29 December I went for a check-up. The nurse examined me and said that I was ready.

She told me to return the next day with my little suitcase and they would induce me. Now I began to feel a little scared. On Saturday afternoon, at 5pm, I was admitted to hospital. The nurse told me what was going to happen the next day. I would need to get up at 5am, have a bath and then they would break my waters, which should start off labour. It all sounded very scary. I just couldn't believe that I would be having a little person coming out of me.

The next day, after I'd got up early, bathed and had my waters broken, Darren and I were wandering around the ward and I couldn't help but think to myself, Surely something should be happening. I asked the nurse if she could tell if my baby was going to be small as the doctors had been worried about this a few months previously.

She felt my stomach and said, 'Well, maybe just a little, but not to worry, as they have all the necessary equipment there if they need it.'

Just after 1pm the contractions started. I could never, ever have imagined such pain – it was definitely not what we had seen in the antenatal video. I was begging Darren to make the pain stop. I kept throwing up into little cardboard bowls that looked like upside-down bowler hats. I desperately needed water, but it tasted like bath water, which, I really do believe, made me throw up even more.

Two hours later, which apparently is very quick, I had given birth to my daughter. She was a big baby, ten pounds, and had caused quite a lot of damage on her arrival. By now all sorts of doctors were popping into the ward to have a look at me, and one of them told me that I needed to go down to theatre to have stitches. I immediately had visions of them wheeling me down the corridors with my legs still high up in the stirrups, but I couldn't do anything about it as I was too weak. They didn't do that, but instead moved me on to a trolley and covered me up. I kept falling asleep while in theatre, where I had loads of stitches and was later taken back to the ward to be reunited with my new daughter. We didn't have a name for her as we'd both been certain that she was going to be a boy. A few days later we took our baby home.

It was nerve-racking at first, but, like all new parents, we soon settled into it. As Darren had to get up at 4am, little Sophie slept with me. She did have her own cot, but I liked her near me. I loved being a mum and tried to concentrate 24 hours a day on my daughter, but my mother kept entering my thoughts. How could my natural mother just leave me? I saw my daughter as being the most precious little thing ever. And then I thought, How could my stepmother hurt a little baby? How could anyone?

During my pregnancy I had decided to breastfeed my baby. I would love to be able to say that I made the decision as it was the healthiest choice, but I was really scared to bottle-feed. What if I made them too hot, too cold, or added too much powder? I already had a million other things to worry about, and breastfeeding meant there was one less. One night, when Sophie was just a few weeks old, I was feeding her and her little face was looking up at me. For the first time ever I felt truly loved and needed. I also felt that maybe I wasn't such a bad person after all. Sophie was the first grandchild on Darren's side, so she was obviously spoiled. One thing I couldn't stand was watching his mum giving Sophie her bottle: it made me feel like second-best and I couldn't have that.

I loved being a mum so much that I wanted another baby right away. It meant that I would have to sleep with Darren, which was a pity, as I had hoped to use my 'giving-birth injuries' excuse for quite a few months. Five months later I was pregnant again. I was a lot calmer this time and once again there were no problems over the term of the pregnancy. In October we moved to a large housing association flat in West Ealing. One afternoon Darren, Sophie and I were walking round the town when we decided to pop into the Register Office to find out what we would need to do to book a wedding. We had briefly talked about it, but nothing definite was ever said. I had always said that I would never get married, but now that I had Sophie I wanted her to have a proper family. I also wanted to have the same surname as her. While we were there we were told that there had been a cancellation, so, if we wanted to, we could get married the following Monday. We said yes and paid the deposit before we could change our minds.

So, the following Monday, we popped down to the town hall with Kim and Darren's mate Steve as our witnesses. We didn't tell our families. It was such short notice that we didn't even have rings. Darren even had to go to work on our wedding night. A few weeks later we told our families. Darren's were a little disappointed and my dad said he felt I had snubbed him, but I knew I would never be able to stand up in front of everyone with all their eyes on me. I just couldn't do that.

Christmas Day came and Sophie was spoiled rotten. She was walking three or four steps by now. She never crawled, as I would never put her down on the floor, scared that she would roll over and bang her head. One week later, on her birthday, she was running round all over the place.

My second baby was due on 8 February. As the day came nearer, snow set in and there was a lot of it. I was too frightened to go out; first, in case I fell and, second, because my first baby had been born so quickly, I had visions of giving birth in the supermarket. The due date, a Friday, came and went. After waking early on Saturday morning with a few pains in my stomach, I turned over and tried to get back to sleep. A few hours later it occurred to me that they might be contractions, so I timed them: they were only three minutes apart. Luckily Karen had been staying the night, but I rang Darren, then Ela and Kim. I wouldn't set off for the hospital until they all were here: three of my most trusted people to look after Sophie as this was the first time I would be leaving her. We left at 7am, with plenty of fresh water. At the hospital the reception nurse was very calm and seemed to take ages. Name? Date of birth? Address? Due date? Finally I got in and again most of the birth was spent with me throwing up into the little cardboard hats.

At 9.21 I had given birth to my son: ten pounds six. James had a few minor health worries and later was occasionally admitted to hospital. There is nothing worse than looking at your baby when he or she is ill and not being able to do anything. When James was eight months old they found out what the problem was and said they could now keep it under control. We decided that we would not have any more children just yet.

Darren was now sorting mail on the night shift, so I could sleep with both my babies. We had a great time together.

Everything I had ever wanted to do as a child, I did with my babies. I really appreciated every moment that I had with them. But I was always scared that they would be taken away from me. As they got older we would go to Thorpe Park and Chessington and we would go swimming, play in the local park or go to the cinema. Christmas time was brilliant: the decorations would go up on the last day of November and every bit of wall space in the living room was filled with Santas or snowmen. The first time I went to the toy store I had to go back and get another trolley, as I filled one up so quickly. I really wanted Sophie and James to have the best childhood ever. We would have games days and eat a picnic meal on the floor. Cheese spreads now had a red strip and when you pulled it the whole wrapper would come off. I couldn't help thinking that this would have been handy on one of my food-stealing trips to the fridge when I was younger. Even though we were having a great time, thoughts like that kept entering my mind. One Pancake Day I suddenly realised that I didn't ever remember having pancakes when I was younger. All these little things that I had missed out on as a child kept filling my thoughts, and it made me feel a bit sad.

Karen had just left school and been offered a job as a live-in nanny. She accepted the position because she had fallen out with my dad over her choice of boyfriends and needed to get away. Currently she was dating a Jamaican and my dad hated it. Karen's new job was to look after a small boy and girl who were just a few months older than my two. The children became good friends over the years. Karen would bring them over and we would have days out together. They would sleep over at my house or my children would sleep with them at theirs, even though their mum, Elaine, used to laugh at me for ringing up all the time to check up on them.

When Sophie started at her nursery it was very hard leaving her there. For the first few weeks I was allowed to stay with her, but was then politely informed that I should go. When she started primary school she hated me leaving her. Sophie was a very shy girl, but she would scream and cry her eyes out. Again I was told to just go, but it was very hard to leave her in that state. All I could think as I walked home was: What is she thinking of me, leaving her like that? I noticed there were tears in the corners of my eyes.

When it was James's turn to start at the nursery, he too hated being left there. Again I walked home in tears. This time I was keenly aware that I didn't have any little hands to hold. With both children now away during the day, I began to worry about their safety. I spent as much time as possible helping out the teacher, though I wasn't really helping her: I was keeping an eye on my kids. I would go in to help them with their reading and was always available on every school trip. I wanted Sophie and James to be able to defend themselves when they were older, so I enrolled them in judo lessons. James didn't like it and quit straight away, but Sophie stuck it out for a few years.

Things were going pretty smoothly until one day I read in the newspaper that a paedophile nicknamed Catweazle (his real name was Leslie Bailey) had been killed in prison. A member of a gang of paedophiles, he had been convicted of killing a small boy. I couldn't believe it. I really did find it hard to believe that these people could actually make contact with other perverts and commit their crimes together. I had always imagined a paedophile as being a dirty old man in a raincoat. But these people weren't ashamed of what they were and went around snatching little kiddies to satisfy their sick and twisted needs. While collecting my kids that day I had a good look at the school's railings and gates. Someone could easily jump over and grab my kids. But why would they run the risk of being seen? I didn't know how far a sicko would go to satisfy his needs. With DNA testing it is so easy to trace the culprit, yet they still do it. I was now very worried.

Darren had come off night duty and with both the kids now at school it was decided that they should have their own bedroom. We decorated the room and the kids moved in. At least they had each other and I wasn't leaving them solely on their own. But I didn't like it. With every single noise I heard I had to get up and check all the doors and windows. I couldn't sleep as I imagined people breaking in to snatch my kids. When I did fall asleep I would have nightmares, mainly about people being nice one minute and then turning into evil monsters the next.

I now began to drink very heavily again. While pregnant and breastfeeding I had stopped, but later on I did occasionally buy a bottle. The trouble was that I could never have just one or two drinks, but had to get drunk. Now, after one or two, I felt I could fight off anybody who dared come near my flat. I even felt brave enough to face my stepmother. The next morning I would feel so bad. What if someone had broken in? I wouldn't have been able to do a thing about it, although probably I would have been too drunk to have even heard them. I went to my GP and told her my worries. She sent me to a mental health clinic, where I spoke to a doctor about all my fears.

Unfortunately, this doctor was eastern European and had trouble understanding me, though she was very professional. I found it very hard to get the words out even once, but to be asked to repeat them was just asking too much of me. She prescribed me sleeping tablets, which I didn't take. I really didn't see the point in replacing what I regarded, perhaps wrongly, as one addiction with another. I went back a few times but didn't find the sessions very useful. I decided to go just one more time and, while I was sitting in reception, I noticed the mother of one of Sophie's school friends. From the way she was chatting with the receptionist, it was obvious she worked there, and I had to hide around the corner. That was my last visit. I just couldn't go back and run the risk of bumping into her. Even though she was a lovely friendly lady, I just felt that I would be labelled 'crazy' and mothers would stop their kids from playing with mine. I knew I wasn't crazy. I was just so unsure about things.

I stopped reading newspapers and never watched the news. I didn't really have a social life, as I was never very comfortable in the outside world. If ever my friends or Karen wanted to catch up with me, they would have to come to the flat. The only place I would ever go to was my dad's, where I would most definitely get drunk. He still charged me 35p for a drink, but this was very generous of him, as he hadn't put his prices up for quite a few years.

Darren didn't like going round to my dad's as he knew that my dad and I would end up drunk and he really didn't want the kids to see either of us in that state. He didn't like my dad, but, if ever he said anything against him, I would automatically jump to my dad's defence. Generally Darren and I got on OK, though he didn't like me drinking and we would constantly argue about it. What he didn't realise was that, if he wanted a sex life with me, I had to drink. Looking back, I'm amazed that I didn't trust the world but still took my children around to my dad's.

NINE

Our flat was the ground floor of a Victorian house that was falling apart. One day cracks started appearing in the ceiling of our living room. The maintenance men tried to jack up the ceiling but then cracks started to appear in the walls. A new ceiling was needed. The kids and I moved into my dad's for a few weeks while the work was carried out. One Monday night Newcastle were playing Manchester United. Even though I had lived in London all my life, I had always been a Newcastle fan, so I put on my football top and watched the match. Bloody Cantona scored and we lost 1–0. As usual, my dad was drunk by 10.30, when he started telling me about my real mum.

'Your mum was from Newcastle, you know,' were his exact words.

That came right out of the blue. I can only imagine that my football shirt must have triggered something off in him.

'No, I didn't know that,' I replied.

'Yeah. That's why I first started chatting to her.' My dad's dad was from Sunderland, right next to Newcastle.

'But I thought she was from Devon,' I said.

'No. They moved there because your mum's dad was really sick. He had been a captain in the Navy but now was really ill and so it was decided that a complete rest and fresh air were the best thing for him. So they moved from one side of the country to the other.'

I decided that while my dad was in this chatty mood I would try to get some more information out of him. He had been a policeman in London but had moved down to Devon to be with his girlfriend. She dumped him and then he met my stepmother Deidre, got her pregnant and married her. They went on to have three baby boys, and my dad had been promoted to the CID when he met my real mum, who was a barmaid at the time. She already had a daughter and was living with her mother, who had just lost her husband, my granddad. She fell pregnant with me almost instantly. (Apparently I was conceived in the back of a van, which my dad found highly amusing.) My dad was asked to leave the police force – he wouldn't tell me why – and moved back to Greenford with his wife and three boys. My real mum was to follow shortly. My dad got her a flat in Ealing but my stepmother found out and went crazy. Dad was not allowed to see my mum any more.

'How did you end up with me then?' I asked.

'Deidre went to see your mum and the next thing we were picking you up from hospital.'

I didn't quite know how to handle all this new information. At first I was immensely angry with my dad, because I had repeatedly begged him for years for any information like this. He knew that I had been looking in Devon and he had never pointed out that my mother was actually from the North-East. The Salvation Army actually came around to see if I had any more information about her, and my dad answered the door and was very friendly and chatty towards them but told them nothing except that he had met her in Devon. I was happy that I now had somewhere else to look. If she wasn't still there, I could at least maybe trace her history, just find out something about her. I really did need to know why she gave me up.

With the work on our flat nearly completed, I couldn't wait to get out of my dad's. The last few nights I spent avoiding him, which Ela noticed and asked me what the problem was. I told her and her response was: 'Your father loves you all very much. He doesn't mean to hurt you.'

My dad could do no wrong in her eyes. Even when my brother Paul, who was working in France, was very ill, I asked my dad what he was going to do.

'What can I do?' was his pathetic reply. 'I can't stop work and go all the way over to France.'

Yeah, 'cos it really is a long way away, I thought to myself. Even when Paul was transferred to the local hospital, right here in Ealing, my dad rarely went to see him. If ever either of my kids were in trouble I would travel to the end of the world to be with them, but my dad never felt like that. I think he saw us kids as a burden on him and it was us that prevented him from doing what he really wanted to do: go to work and then go to the pub and be one of the boys.

The kids and I returned home. Darren was on nights again and so went to bed after tea, to try to get a few hours' kip before he had to go in. I had been brooding over my dad's revelations for long enough and decided that I was going to give my search for Mum one last try. I was going to go to the Births, Deaths and Marriages office and try to get her date of birth and then go back to the Salvation Army and see if they could help. I rang the office and got through to a security guard who told me to come over and have a look. He told me that it should be fairly easy to trace her as long as we had a rough age for her.

The following day I took Sophie and James to school, walked down to Ealing Broadway, paid for my ticket and jumped on the Tube. By two o'clock that afternoon I had returned home with my mother's birth and marriage details. I had found out that I had two younger sisters and had ordered their birth certificates, which would be arriving in a few days. It had all been so easy. I estimated Mum was about 18 when she had me, so I just went back to 1950 (I was born in 1968) and started searching through the books. There were four books for each year and they were all listed alphabetically, so I just had to look up her name. When I finished one year I just went back a year; having such an unusual surname made her easy to find. There she was in the book for those born in 1946, and the entry even gave her father's occupation as Navy captain.

Ten minutes it had taken me. Then I decided to see if she ever married, so I went to 1968 and started going through the books again. In 1972 she had married a man called Paul Schrouder. Again it had been very easy, so I thought I'd see if they'd had any children. First I got Alice's details, as I knew her name and roughly what year she was born; it was very easy. She appeared in the 1965 entries. Now all I needed to do was to look for any Schrouder children. I started with 1969. Going by my mum's first two children, she obviously didn't need to be married to have kids. In the 1975 book I found Clare and in the 1977 one I found Wendy. Clare had been my middle name and I did wonder if she was named after me. It had all been so easy. I was so lucky that both Mum's maiden and married names had been unusual ones. I was happy that she had married and had some more babies, babies that she could actually keep. I ordered all the certificates and went back home.

Darren was awake when I got in. I think he was a little upset at being left out of my discovery, but we had tried many times before. We had constantly gone to the Citizens Advice Bureau, but because I wasn't legally adopted there was nothing anyone could do. I told him all my news and he was a bit gobsmacked by it all. A few days later the certificates arrived. I felt a little numb. In my hands I had all this official paperwork about my family and yet they probably didn't even know I existed. Mum, her husband and their last child were all born in the North-East. I began to piece together her life. She had come down to Devon with her parents, had given birth to Alice, met my dad, moved to London, given birth to me, met and married her husband, had their first child and then maybe moved back home and had their second child. I decided that the next thing to do would be to check out phone books, starting off in the North-East, the other end of the country from where I'd been looking until then. Darren came with me and we soon found a few Schrouders; we also found a couple of A. Doonies (Alice's name) – I thought that if I couldn't find Mum I would try to find Alice. One of the Schrouders we found had the same initials as Mum's husband, P.M., but no Kathleen Schrouder appeared. We decided to stick to P.M. Schrouder and now we needed to know if it was our guy or not.

In London we asked how we could check the electoral register for North-East England. A man took our details and made a phone call. Yes, it was Mum's husband, and he was living there but she wasn't; either that or she just wasn't registered. Maybe they were divorced, or maybe she wasn't registered so she could dodge the council tax. Or maybe she was dead. I should have checked the Death records while I was there, but things were going so well I didn't want to think negatively. I was now in a checkmate situation. We went back home happy that we did at least have some concrete evidence of Mum. She was alive, I decided. But, as much as I would have loved to hear her voice, I couldn't call her. It would have been too much of a shock. Darren would have to do it. But then how would Paul like strange men ringing up enquiring about his wife. It had to be Darren. We decided that the coming Saturday night he would call.

He took me and the kids round to my dad's. (England played Poland and we won 2–0.) I was a nervous wreck. I must have chain-smoked all evening and when I didn't have a cigarette in my mouth I had a drink there. The phone rang, I shot out to answer it and it was Darren. He had called and got through to Paul and, yes, they were divorced.

'Who did you say you were?' I asked Darren.

'Well, I asked for Kathleen and said that I was ringing on behalf of her daughter.'

'Wendy?' Paul asked.

'No.'

'Clare?'

'No.'

'Alice?'

'No.'

'Oh, the other one?'

'Yes.'

'Well, she's babysitting tonight, so call this number after 8pm.'

'Thanks.'

'Oh, my God,' I said. 'You're actually going to be talking to my mum in a couple of hours' time.'

I couldn't believe it. I was so nervous. It was such a big thing, finding my mum, I found it hard to believe that it was real. In the back of my mind there was always the possibility that she would say, 'Go away.' But at least I would know and could finally move on. Those two hours seemed like ages. I managed to down quite a few more vodkas with one eye constantly on the clock. Eight o'clock. I knew he wouldn't ring until half-time. At 8.45 the phone rang.

'Well, I spoke to her,' Darren said. 'She was very shocked but said that deep down she knew this day would come. She asked how you were and said she was glad that you're happily married with your own family. I asked her if you could write and she said yes and gave me her address. Then she said goodbye.'

I had finally done it. I didn't know what to say or do. My thoughts went back to me lying in my bed the day before my birthday, thinking about how I would react if I ever got a birthday card from my own mum. Now I was just numb.

'What did she sound like?' I asked.

'She was well-spoken, with a strong Geordie accent,' Darren said. 'And she lives in the middle of Newcastle.'

I didn't tell my dad or anyone else just yet, because, even though Mum had said that I could write to her, I still knew she could easily change her mind. I woke Darren at 3am the next morning, just to get him to tell me again what she'd said.

I did write to her that very night, although immediately I was faced with a problem. What do I call her? Kathleen? Mrs Schrouder? Mum? Miss Doonie? I decided on Kathleen. I told her about Sophie and James, a bit about my past and what I'd done with my life. I told her that I'd always known about Alice and had found out about Clare and Wendy a few days previously. Darren rewrote the letter because my writing is so bad that she would never have been able to read it. It was posted and she would get it on Tuesday.

I woke on Wednesday and thought maybe I'd get a reply today, but no, it really was too soon. Maybe tomorrow. Thursday came, but no letter. Darren kept telling me to just relax and not be so impatient. Friday morning came and we didn't get a postman at all. He would normally go up the other side of the road, cross over and then come back down. We used to see him most mornings on our way to school, but today there was no sign of him. At 1.45 the letter was delivered. Our normal postie had gone sick and our round had to be done as overtime. I noticed the Newcastle postmark. I had a letter from my mum. I just stood and stared at it for a few seconds. The postie must have thought I was crazy. I tore it open.

She said that she had left me with my dad as she thought this was for the best. She mentioned that he had contacted her while she was in Devon and told her that he was now divorced with six children. Again that angry little flame started to flicker. All this time I had been begging my dad for any information he had on her, but I got nothing from him. I also felt a little hurt that my mum hadn't tried to contact me once she knew that Deidre was gone. She had told Clare and Wendy about me, although I was a little disappointed that they didn't already know and they were very keen to contact me. She would love it if I called her 'Mum', she wrote, and said she was known by her middle name, Pat. That wasn't even one of my options when I was searching for her! She ended the letter with: 'I would like to think you had a happy childhood.'

I went to pick the kids up and saw Sophie through her classroom door. I pointed to my letter and smiled. She knew and smiled back. I was just so happy. I couldn't stop smiling all the time and quite often I felt the urge to put my arms in the air and just yell, 'YES!'

We had booked a holiday for the following week. From Saturday, 13 June we were going to spend two weeks in Cornwall. On the Thursday before we were due to go, the phone rang. Darren and I looked at each other. We both knew. Darren answered and then passed me the phone. 'It's your mum,' he said.

He took the kids out of the room and left me alone to chat with her. It was a very strange conversation. She started off by telling me that she really thought that her giving me up had been for the best. It was very hard to understand what she was saying as she spoke in such a strong Geordie accent. As a result there were quite a few pauses when she had asked me a question and was waiting for an answer but I hadn't been able to understand her. I was just so happy to hear her voice. I was also shaking and kept stuttering, which I was very annoyed about. Just be calm, I kept saying to myself. She did say that there must be things that I needed to know. But I said no. I really did think that the past now didn't matter. Forwards not backwards. But of course I did need answers, which was probably the main reason why I needed to find her. She said I could call her when I got back from my holiday.

Deep down I had always imagined Mum out there somewhere, missing me just like I missed her, and when I found out that she'd got on with her life I was truly happy for her, while also feeling a little hurt and neglected.

Two days later we drove down to Cornwall. Even though it rained every single day we still had a great time. It really didn't matter what we were doing just as long as we were together. Sophie and I went swimming every single morning, which was a good kick-start to the diet and fitness plan I had set for myself. I loved seeing my kids laugh and have fun. They were what mattered. No matter how much I loved having a mum, I had to be really careful that my two children never felt neglected. I was a mother first and a daughter second. Unfortunately for Darren, being a wife was very low down on my list. We returned home to hear the upsetting news that my nan had fallen over and was in hospital.

Darren knew that I was keen to ring my mum, so he took the kids round to his dad's. After a couple of vodkas I rang my mum. I had to smile every time I said the words: 'my mum'.

She did answer a lot of my questions, although some of her answers I wasn't too keen on hearing. She had moved to Devon with her parents and had fallen pregnant with Alice. Her father was a strict Irish (that means that I'm 25 per cent Irish) Catholic, but he had died without knowing about his daughter's pregnancy. Mum was in an institute for 'unmarried mothers' when she gave birth to Alice. Her mother, as she had just lost her husband, agreed to raise Alice. But my mum saw her as much as possible and took on two jobs to pay for her upkeep. She then met my dad and, at first, didn't know that he was married. She just knew that he was high up in the police force and started a relationship with him. I'm not sure if she then fell pregnant with me before he took her back to his house, but he did take her there and showed her his three boys. They were all still in cots as there is only a year between each of us. Paul, my nearest brother, had to be kept in hospital for six weeks after his birth as he had caught whooping cough. It all seemed so heartless.

I also felt that it was no wonder that Deidre, my stepmother, had hated me. After all, I was my mother's daughter – and my father's. I asked how they ended up with me and she told me that it was Deidre who had wanted me but only if I was a girl and if a blood test proved that I was actually my dad's. I got the impression that my real mum didn't really like my stepmother. Once my mum had moved to Ealing, my dad stopped all contact with her, and I guessed this was about the time when his wife had found out.

'Once I had given birth to you I rang them and they appeared on the hospital steps,' my mum explained. 'The nurse handed you to me and I handed you to Deidre. She did tell me that she was going to call you Susan Clare.' We carried on chatting and talked about a possible visit. I said yes but not yet – I was massively overweight and didn't want her to meet me until I'd lost some of it. She was remarrying on Wednesday. She had been going out with a man called Glynn and they had set a date. I wished her luck and we said goodbye.

I rang my sister Karen and told her all my news. I also told her that, even though I had three more sisters now, she was always my real one. She was fine about things and said that she had always known how much I had wanted to find my mum.

Over the next few days I began to ponder about things. Mum kept saying that she left me with my dad as it was for the best. I couldn't understand how she could leave me there with someone that she didn't really like. Also, what sort of family life was that going to be for me with a cheating father? He had done it once, so there was always the possibility that he would again. It wasn't the most stable family to have left me with. Why did she carry on having an affair with him after she had seen his babies in their cots? What did she want from him? Was she expecting him to leave his wife and family? I kept saying to myself, It's all in the past, just forget about it. But deep down I felt that I had suffered all of those beatings because of my mum and dad's behaviour.

I had spoken to my new sisters a few times now and seemed to get on OK with them.

A week before my twenty-eighth birthday my nan passed

away. I had always loved and respected her. She was great. My nan outlived all her children, made it through two world wars, had been burgled twice, had fallen over and broken her hip but had bounced back every time. And now one silly little fall and she was gone. I was very upset. I thought that she would live for ever.

I will always remember the last Christmas Day that I spent with my nan. Karen was pregnant, Steven was dating Nita and Uncle Wal had spent Christmas with Nan. They had all spent the evening round at my dad's. Uncle Wal was Bet's husband. Bet, my nan's last surviving child, had recently died, so this was Uncle Wal's first Christmas without her. Uncle Wal had drunk a few drinks and was a bit wobbly, so Karen and I decided to take him and my nan back home. Unfortunately, Uncle Wal fell and cut his head and had to go to hospital. Karen and Steven went with him and I stayed with my nan, who was naturally very worried about her son-in-law.

'Right, Nan,' I said. 'Where are these photo albums?'

My nan had loads of photos, which I had always loved looking at. They went back many years. She showed me some pictures of her when she was a young girl, when Greenford was mainly fields. She told me many stories, like the time when King George VI went through Greenford in his carriage and how excited everyone was to see him. I loved Nan's stories. She showed me photo after photo of people that she had known and loved. I looked at her: she was having a great time. She remembered everything as if it was yesterday.

I'm sorry that Uncle Wal hurt his head, but I am grateful that I got to spend my nan's last Christmas with her.

My birthday was on the Tuesday after Nan died. I finally got a card from my mum. At last! I also received a photo of her and my sisters, which had been taken at her recent wedding. They all looked so young and pretty. I automatically felt down. There was no way that I could have been in that picture and not stuck out like a sore thumb. I was, and always had been, a jeans and T-shirt person. I never wore jewellery, make-up or pretty clothes. But I was happy that I had got my birthday card.

Darren always made a fuss of me on birthdays because he knew that I would always be thinking of my mum on this day. When the kids were a few years old he got them to put some candles on a cake. My first birthday cake. It was great to have my own family and I wished that I could've just forgotten about my mum but I couldn't. I don't know why.

Two days later was my nan's funeral. My auntie from the Isle of Wight came up for it and when she heard about my news she told me, 'Don't ever forget about your dad now. He's been good to you.'

'Of course not. I could never forget my dad,' was my reply.

I got very drunk that day. My brothers and I were talking about the dreaded stepmother. I think my news about my mum must have triggered off their own memories. Anthony told me that he had contacted her a few years previously. Why? I asked him.

'I just wanted to know if she'd changed. But she hadn't. She didn't ask anything about me, she just talked about her two other sons. She never bothered to call me back, so I just left it,' he said.

I think hearing that Anthony had contacted his mother, and

we all knew how awful she was, made it a little clearer why I needed to trace my mum. I felt that having a mum would be the answer to all my problems. Just like when I was a little girl and I would dream about her coming to take me away and we would live happily ever after.

I spoke to my new sisters quite a few times over the next few months. I thought that I would be closest to Alice, who was also semi-left by my mum, but it was Clare that I got on really well with. I asked her all sorts of questions about my mum but I could never say just 'mum': it was always 'your mum'. I didn't want them thinking that I was taking anything away from them.

Over the next few months I felt very anxious. I lost a massive amount of weight in a very short time. I would sit next to the phone, just in case she rang. My stomach was so knotty that I couldn't eat. I was still smoking and drinking. I kept on saying to myself, If she doesn't like me, so what? I have Darren, Sophie and James (even though I was planning on divorcing Darren just as soon as the kids were old enough). Sophie and James truly loved me, but then all kids loved their parents. I even loved mine!

In the first letter that my mum sent me, she had said, 'I would like to think you had a happy childhood.' I didn't really know what I was going to say about that. My body has scars all over. I don't have mirrors in my house as the first thing I see when I look into it is the scar just above my top lip. This was when she punched me and her ring had caught me. I never like to look at myself as it's a constant reminder that I am a shitface.

I had spoken to my mum a few times and it had been arranged for me to visit them all up in Newcastle in October. I had decided to go by coach as there was no way I could have driven, even though I really wanted to, because with my lack of sense of direction I would most certainly have got lost. Also I felt I would probably be too nervous to drive, so a 300-mile journey would not be the best thing for me to do. And I never liked trains, so a coach it was. I would be leaving Victoria at 9am on Sunday and would arrive in Newcastle at 3pm to meet my mum.

TEN

The Saturday before, I was all prepared. I had lost a massive amount of weight and had gone down three sizes. I had spent the past few months working out to a Rosemary Conley video. I didn't want my mum to be ashamed or embarrassed of me. I did tell her during a phone call that I was a little bit scared to meet everyone in case they didn't like me. But she said exactly the same about me. I thought to myself that there was absolutely no way that I would ever dislike my mum. How could I? She was my mum.

I was worried, though, for having a mum was now a reality, whereas before it was just a dream. Sometimes dreams can be built up so high that reality doesn't stand a chance. Surprisingly enough, I was fairly calm. I went to bed early but couldn't sleep. I kept remembering back to my teens, when I would look at my friends' mums and secretly wish that I had a mum like theirs. I didn't want to drink as I really didn't want to be a bleary-eyed mess the next day. I knew that, if I had just one, two hours later I would be drunk. Eventually, around three-ish, I fell asleep.

Darren and the kids drove me to Victoria. We were early and so had a good wander around. I saw my coach approaching and started to puff away at my last cigarette for six hours. I said goodbye to Darren and kissed the kids goodbye. I sat at the back of the coach and fortunately no one sat next to me — perhaps my frowny look put some people off. I saw Darren and the kids out of the window and for a split second I really wanted to get off the coach and go back home with them. Why was I leaving them to go to the other end of the country to meet a woman who'd abandoned me 28 years ago and not shown any interest in me since? I had to do this and I knew that I would regret it if I didn't. If things didn't turn out well, at least I would know the truth.

I was a little surprised at how calm I was. I had been so nervous for months and now here I was quite peaceful. I think that once the coach set off it was out of my hands. I would be meeting my mum in a few hours. I settled down to the long journey. The coach pulled in to Newcastle at 2.30. I was glad we were early as I'd had visions of me falling down the coach steps in front of my mum in my nervousness. I got off, got my bags and found a quite corner to settle down in and have a smoke. Gallowgate coach station was very different to Victoria. After ten minutes the place had emptied and I was all by myself. I slipped into the ladies' just to make sure that I didn't have any hideous stains on my face or a chunk of hair wasn't standing on end. No, I was fine.

Then I went outside and waited. While I was standing there

I noticed a large stadium directly over the road from me. I couldn't believe it. It was St James' Park, the home of my beloved Newcastle United. If I didn't support Newcastle, I thought, I would not have worn their football shirt and my dad would not have told me about my mum and I would not be standing here waiting to meet her. Strange the way things turn out.

I saw a car pull in. Yep, it was her. I recognised her from the photo. I stepped round a corner, bunged a few mints into my mouth as I didn't want to have smoky breath and waited for her to come over.

'Sue, is that you?'

I was kneeling down trying desperately to do up a zip on my bag, which all of a sudden had refused to budge.

I stood up and said, 'Hi.' I was now facing her and automatically I looked down. I had always had trouble looking people straight in the face.

She opened up her car door and I put my bags in. I couldn't look at her, as much as I wanted to.

'What are you thinking?' she asked. 'Is there anything you want to say?'

'I don't know,' I said.

She nodded and said, 'That's OK.'

I did try to sneak a sideways glance, but I couldn't do it. I was sitting in the car with my real mum for the first time and didn't know what to say or do. She lived only ten minutes away, in a two-bedroom maisonette with her new husband, and once we got there she showed me my room. It was her spare bedroom, which she used for Oliver, her grandson, and it was also her smoking room, as she didn't like to smoke around her husband, who had recently given it up. I felt a little relieved to be given my own space, but as I looked up I saw that she had put up on the walls all the photos that I had sent her. I saw Sophie and James and realised how much I missed them. I went into the living room and my mum said that we'd be going to Alice's later. I was relieved as I thought I'd automatically click with Alice because Mum had also given her away.

The two things I noticed most about my first visit to Newcastle were, first, I couldn't understand a word anybody said to me and, second, it was freezing. We went to Alice's home, up on the Northumberland coast, where I met her and her boyfriend, Adam. They were so warm and friendly, they really did make me feel welcome, and I felt they were totally genuine people. Now that there were others about I could take a good look at my mum. Claudette used to tease me and say that I had a 'ski-slope' nose and as I looked at my mum I could see where I got it. I liked having something in common with her. The Hamfords had all been blue-eyed blondes but I was green-eyed with brown hair – again just like my mum.

The evening went well. Alice got out her photos and I saw relatives past and present. It was fun. Later on Clare turned up. She had recently split from her husband and arrived with her boyfriend, Billy, and her one-year-old son, Oliver. She came over and gave me a hug – the first person apart from my children that I'd actually hugged – and said something that I couldn't make out at all. Clare was great. They were all so friendly. My mum – I could say it in my head – could see that I was having trouble understanding and told Clare to slow down. Now the room was full I could take long glances at my mum, just like I felt she was doing to me. The next day she and I went out for lunch. The whole meal was spent in total silence. I just couldn't think of anything to say.

Wendy, my college friend, had recently met her natural mother and I'd asked her what they had had to talk about. She said they just talked about everything, it came naturally, and she was surprised how well they got on.

I racked my brains as to what to say to my mum. I couldn't talk about the Hamford family. I couldn't talk about my two as I felt that she might get offended if I started going on about how much I loved my babies. Would I be rubbing salt into the wounds? Did she have any wounds? To me giving up a baby would be the most heart-breaking decision ever. I was starting to feel that she had already given up one, and even though she did still occasionally see her, was it hard for her? Did she regret it? Deep down I was seeing it as the easy option. Easy for her. She did say that giving up a baby was the hardest thing ever and apparently she did come back to visit a few times, but she had to let go. I can't judge her, as I have never been in that kind of situation. I do sometimes feel that after having Alice she could have been a bit more careful but it was the sixties, a completely different era. She had been sent to a convent from the age of three and had a very strict father. So, once an adult, she went out and had fun.

On the whole the visit had been OK. It was hard seeing my mum being a mother to my sisters, but I would rather have had them there than be alone with my mum in total silence. We had been out a few times but, because of my 'soft southern blood',

I absolutely froze. I had never been so cold in all my life and it was only October. Mum took me back to the coach station. We had a few minutes to wait.

She told me, 'Seeing you there for the first time was like turning the clock back 30 years, you're so like your father.'

I didn't really like that as I wanted her to like me for myself and not because I reminded her of her past boyfriend. We said our goodbyes and I returned to London.

When I arrived home that evening I heaved a big sigh of relief. I had achieved my childhood goal. I hoped we would keep in contact but if I never saw my mum again that would be OK, for now at least I knew she was all right. It was great to be back with my kids. I had missed them so much.

Mum and I kept in contact and we arranged for her to come and visit me in December. I went to collect her from Victoria. We seemed to get on a lot better this time. The first time we had met it had been very difficult to speak freely in case either of us said the wrong thing. I sometimes felt that I was walking on eggshells, but now we were more at ease with each other. She met Darren and the kids. Both my children are immensely shy but normally Sophie leads the way and James follows. But Sophie was very, very quiet with my mother. My dad invited us round to his house for dinner. Over the past few months I had talked to Ela about my mum and she was very keen to meet her. I said yes to her request because I remembered the embarrassing silences that occurred when it was just my mum and I together.

We arrived at my dad's and I rang the bell. He answered.

'Dad, this is Mum. Mum, this is Dad.' I actually said those words. They shook hands, which I thought was extremely funny.

The evening went well. Mum and Ela got on great and were chatting, laughing and even, after quite a few drinks, dancing with each other. We were invited round again the following night. During the evening the conversation turned to my stepmother, Deidre.

'I think you're a weak man and should have stopped her beating Susan,' my mum told my dad. Yes! Mum is sticking up for me, I thought.

'Well, what could I do? If I had stopped her then she may have started on the boys,' was Dad's weak reply.

'Oh, I didn't know,' said Mum.

'And anyway, she was good to Susan at first. She didn't start breaking her bones or pulling her ears off until a few years later,' said my dad, making comical movements with his hands.

They both laughed. Ela looked at me, shocked, and told my dad to shut up. Too late. My mum and dad had both just laughed at me. I didn't think it was funny. The evening went from bad to worse. I went to the other end of the room and lay on the floor chatting with Sophie and James. When I went up to the bar to get myself another drink, my mum and dad both told me to go away. They were talking about the good old days. My mum said that because she lived near a naval base she could say, 'No, not tonight' in several different languages.

'But not in English,' I replied. I couldn't help it. Earlier on we had been driving around Ealing so that she could remember things and all I got was: 'I used to date a lad from there' or 'I remember that place – so and so took me there.' I didn't like to ask if she was pregnant with me at the time or if it was just after she had left me.

I took her to Victoria the next day. On the Tube she suddenly said, 'Oh, is that Wormwood Scrubs?'

'Yes, Mum. Who do you know that's been in there?'

'You'd be surprised.'

I was a little relieved to see her go. I liked her but had to come to terms with the fact that she was not a poor little country girl who had been led astray by a city guy. I had seen a side to her that I didn't want to believe existed: the uncaring side. 'Go away' were her exact words that night.

I rang Ela. She was in a bad way. She told me that my mum and dad had been kissing and heavy petting and when they saw Ela they had also told her to go away. Oh, my God! I felt very responsible. My dad had even been round to my flat that very morning and gone in to see my mum. I don't know what was said, but obviously I never told Ela that. She forgave my dad. As for me, I was determined that he and my mum should never meet again.

Over the next 18 months I met my mum several times. I took the kids up to Newcastle a few times or she would come down, although her going to my dad's was out of the question as far as I was concerned. I was now beginning to get a bit defensive in her company.

One night, while I was cooking the evening meal, she came out and said, 'Oh, you cook your potatoes like that?'

I so wanted to say, 'Well, if I'd had my mum around to show me how to cook them properly, then maybe I wouldn't be cooking them this way!' But I didn't. I did still enjoy having a mum and did not want her to feel bad in any way.

Now that Sophie was eight and James seven, I decided that I should go back to work. For the previous seven years I had been filling envelopes from home. At first it started off as something to do for a few hours in the evening but gradually it took over. I was working 14–16 hours most days for a pathetic £1.50 per hour. At first the money was considered an extra as Darren was on a good wage, but the more I did it the more we relied on it. Then one day I'd had enough. The whole flat was filled with boxes and envelopes and I decided that I was going to go out to work instead. I had enjoyed working for Royal Mail and, as luck would have it, a new International Office was about to open in our area. I applied, passed the interview and was told I could start in three weeks' time, on 6 July 1998.

ELEVEN

I was nervous about my new job but also excited about getting back into the real world. The first two weeks were very boring, mainly classroom stuff, but they soon passed and I settled into my new routine. I worked the late shift, 2pm to 10pm. We thought this was for the best as Darren finished at midday and so one of us would always be there for the children.

At first I liked the fact that I was getting paid for a 40-hour week. I would come home at 10.30 and that was it. Before, I would normally be doing my leaflets until 3 or 4am. Friday nights were the best as I had the whole weekend off after that. I always remember when I was 11 years old, doing my milk round on a Saturday morning, and sometimes kids would answer the door and yell to their mums before going back to their TV programmes. I was so envious of them. I wished I could have a morning off and stay at home and watch TV. And now on Friday nights, with the whole weekend ahead of me, I could put a film on, have a meal (even though eating late was putting back on all the weight I had previously lost), drink and smoke until the early hours of the morning.

Wendy, my youngest Geordie sister, was due to stay with me for a few months as she wanted to work in London and needed somewhere until she sorted herself out. I had to go to my dad's one night because it was his birthday. Once I started going out to work again I'd almost stopped going round there, although it wasn't intentional. Wendy came with me that evening. I had asked Ela if that was OK and she said, 'The more the merrier.' Paul was there with his wife and so were my youngest brother, Steven, and his girlfriend, Nita. True to form, the evening was spent drinking lots. Just before we were about to leave, Paul asked if he could have a word. We went upstairs into the spare room, where he broke down in tears and told me how sorry he was but it was he who had had to tell my stepmother everything that I'd been doing at school. She used to give him sweets as a reward, he said.

I hadn't even suspected Paul; everyone else, but not him. It was so obvious now. I told him not to worry as she had gone and not to waste any more time thinking about it. But I was a little taken aback: not so much that he had confessed, but why. Was it seeing me with my other family? Now that I had a mum, was he thinking about his own mum? Then I had a very nasty thought. What if Steven wanted to trace his mother? He was only 18 months old when she left and so he couldn't have any memories of her. But then he must have heard things from all of us over the years and maybe he was feeling the urge to find her. He was due to marry Nita, who's Hindu and very much into 'the family'. I couldn't tell him not to, for if someone told me not to I wouldn't have listened. If someone had told me that she was the worst person in the world I still would have done it.

Now I began to feel scared. The thought of seeing my stepmother again really terrified me. I was now drinking nearly every night. The nights I wasn't drinking – and that was only because I was too hungover from the previous night – I couldn't sleep. I was having the most horrific nightmares. Not just about me but now also about my children. I was too scared to sleep.

I semi-enjoyed my work. Most weeks I was in the 'rebuts section', where we dealt with 'return to sender' mail and after a while I found myself taking charge of the section. That was OK, but some weeks I was in 'segging' where all I did was pick up a sack of mail, look at the label, put it into one of 12 cages and then do the same thing again 30 seconds later. Great fun! My mind would just go numb and I would be counting down the seconds until the next break. Having a ciggie break was the highlight of my working day. But it was still an improvement on my last job. At least I now had regular pay, holiday pay and a pension, and it was just for eight hours a day. They would play the radio and I started listening to current pop music. I had always been a fan of fifties and sixties music, but now I was introduced to quite a few good more recent singers and groups and started buying their CDs. These I would tape and listen to on my headphones to while away the boring hours. I had a break at 8pm every night and always rang Darren to see if everything was OK.

I greatly missed being at home cooking everyone's tea,

bathing the kids, taking them to bed, reading their bedtime story. Sometimes when I rang Darren he would tell me that they were in the middle of a game and automatically I felt very left out. I kept telling myself that he was their dad and not some stranger, but I really wanted to be there and not wasting my time doing a boring job for which the only purpose to me was a pay cheque. I had to get used to it. Some mums have to work all the hours God sends just to provide for their kids, I told myself. I have to always think of the people that are less fortunate than myself: it just helps me to realise things are not so bad.

All the same, I made quite a few good friends at work, both male and female. It was the female ones who surprised me the most and made me start to question things. I had grown up in a male environment and had always worked in mainly male jobs and so I'd had very little contact with women. One day three female colleagues and I were sitting around a table when the conversation turned to sex. One woman's husband was due home from a trip later that day and she started telling us in detail what she was going to do to him sexually. I was completely shocked. Deep down I had really believed that women didn't enjoy sex but did it simply to satisfy their men. Women who openly enjoyed sex were previously considered sluts, but now it was OK to admit to enjoying it. But were they really enjoying it or were they just boasting? I just assumed that they were boasting, but why would they? I had heard men boast about sex and knew that they were trying to impress their mates, but were women now doing the same? I think that somewhere I knew they weren't, for even in TV shows women were becoming more sexually demanding.

There was something wrong with me, I now realised. I had never enjoyed sex and still used every possible excuse to get out of doing it. Did that mean that I was gay? I never wore make-up or jewellery or even ladies' clothes, so I guess I was probably typecast as being gay. Other people at work certainly assumed I was. The more I thought about it the more distressed I became. I knew I wasn't gay, so what was wrong with me? I was beginning to see myself as some kind of freak.

After six months of working on the floor I heard that a lot of people in the building were failing a test that, if passed, could take them off the Operations floor and into an office job. I decided to try it, just to see if I could pass it. I did, and found it fairly easy. Officially known as the LA (letters administrator) exam, it was three small tests on English and Maths. All of a sudden I was in demand within the building. There were vacancies for support roles in a few departments but the LA exam had to be passed first. I didn't really want an office position as I was happy working in my rebuts section, but that work wasn't always guaranteed because, if they were short-staffed elsewhere in 'Ops', the manager would come and put us in another area: the dreaded 'seg'! So I took the office position. They changed my hours to 10am to 6pm, which meant that I could spend my evenings with my family. I told them that I had two small children and they said if ever they were ill or on school holiday I could change my hours accordingly.

When I told them I had never even used a fax machine, let alone touched a computer, they said, 'No problem. We'll train you.'

They were really great about everything. I was put into Revenue Protection. I was really scared at first as I would have to contact our customers and also quite a few 'high-up' people within Royal Mail. Basically the guys outside would check the mail against the docket and if it didn't match up I needed to speak to the customer to sort out the problem. At first my manager was a middle-aged gentleman who liked things to be done properly. He was OK and showed me how to deal with things. I was beginning to enjoy my new role and before I knew it I was chatting away to the customers and having a laugh with them. I don't know why I was so scared: they were just people like me, doing a job. My office was on the Ops floor, so I could still wander round and go and chat to my mates.

One day I brought in a school photo of my children and placed it against the side of my PC. A top manager saw it and asked whose children they were.

'They're mine,' I answered.

He looked at me and said, 'Really?'

What was he saying? Was it so hard to believe that I had two great kids? I know he didn't mean to, but he really kicked me hard. My drinking was still a regular thing but now it was becoming harder to hide. I had to be in by 10am and most mornings I was very bleary-eyed. I tried everything. I drank gallons of water before I went to sleep, or I would try to wake up early and get a carton of fruit juice down me, but nothing worked. I was taking time off sick and knew that I had got out of control. Every morning now I was waking up with such a feeling of self-hate and worthlessness. I confided in my workmate John, who gave me a number for Royal Mail's

Occupational Health department. I rang them and told them all my problems. They sent a woman round to my house to have a chat. She said she would find me some counselling and would get in touch.

My manager was leaving and so the service liaison manger stepped into his role until a replacement was found. He was great and we got on really well. Unfortunately, though, his name was Vincent, which was still a painful reminder of my childhood injury. I was beginning to have a lot of flashbacks now. Steven was arranging a surprise birthday party for my dad, but for the first time I really didn't want to go. I was starting to have many flashbacks of my dad's abuse and I felt that he had ruined me and that was why I'd never enjoyed sex. Now I was away from him, I was beginning to see him for what he really was. I had always felt grateful to him for taking me in but responsible for my first stepmother leaving. Now I was beginning to realise that it might not have been my fault. Every father should be responsible for raising their kids and I didn't need to feel grateful. I was also feeling very angry.

Despite this, when my dad's birthday came round in September, I went to the party. I couldn't not go and anyway I enjoyed seeing my brothers. Anthony turned up with his partner, Chris, and I absolutely loved him. Andrew came with his three daughters, Karen brought her son Jake, Steven had Nita, but Paul didn't turn up. His wife had left him and he didn't want to be the only one there without a partner. My Auntie Hilary I collected from the airport earlier.

I barely spoke to my dad all evening, but at one point a nasty thought entered my head. Andrew's daughters were running around and was my dad sitting there with an erection? I felt very sick. They were so beautiful and innocent, I couldn't imagine anyone harming them, but I knew that my father was capable of it. I had always believed that he would never touch other little girls as they had brothers or dads themselves and my dad was scared of other men. The only reason that he had friends was because he gave them free drinks. But how could a little girl turn a man on, a father of six? I couldn't understand it and was getting more and more confused.

Soon things were starting to weigh heavily on my mind, and I decided to confide in Kim, who often popped round to my house on a Friday night. I started the conversation off by talking about my stepmother Deidre. Kim also remembered incidents. She told me that she remembered that I was always in my bedroom. She also told me about the time when my stepmother went for her and she remembers hiding behind a chair feeling petrified. I told her that I was looking at maybe going to see a counsellor. After quite a few more drinks I told her all about the abuse I received from my father. She was in total shock. I didn't go into details with her. I didn't really tell anyone exactly what I'd had to do. One step at a time.

The Occupational Health lady had found me a centre that would offer me 12 weeks of free counselling. I had to ring them up and arrange an appointment for an assessment, and we arranged a meeting on 24 November. There I told a lady about everything that had happened and she said that as soon as a vacancy appeared I could have it. It would be on either a Wednesday morning or a Thursday afternoon she said. Secretly

I hoped for the Thursday slot as I could then take the whole afternoon off work. When I'd told John at work that I might need counselling he had looked into my having time off. In my department there were five managers and one of us had to be there on a Saturday, but would then have a day off during the week. Nobody liked doing Saturdays, so it was arranged that during my 12 weeks I would do them and then have a weekday off. If I couldn't do a Saturday, we agreed, I would just make up the hours later on. The other managers were great about the whole thing and I was truly grateful to them. I received a letter from a counsellor at the Open Door project called Susan, who offered me 12 weekly sessions, every Thursday afternoon at 3.30, starting in January.

I might as well give it a go, I said to myself.

But I was still drinking a lot. A few drinks gave me strength, so that I felt I could do anything I wanted to do. I decided that I didn't need counselling. I was going to get through it by myself: I was strong enough. When I told John, he said, 'For Christ's sake, just go, even if it's just the once.'

'OK,' I told him. 'I'll give it a try.'

TWELVE

On the first day of counselling I went to work as normal. I wasn't nervous or anxious at all. My top manager saw me and asked if I was still going. They all knew I was going to counselling but didn't know why.

'Yes, I'm still going. My husband's taking me later.'

'Good,' he said.

I phoned Darren at dinnertime and he asked where I was.

'At work,' I replied.

'Well, I think you should be here as we have to leave in half an hour.'

Damn it. I'd got the time wrong. I thought it was starting at 4.30. I left immediately, but I had to fill the car up on the way home and was starting to feel anxious about being late for my first session. It wouldn't be a good start at all. I got home, had a wash and left again. Darren's dad was going to pick up the kids. I liked him; he was an OK guy. He didn't know where we were going, though. Darren drove me there. I wasn't at all nervous; if anything, I was sort of looking forward to it. I wasn't committed to doing the 12 weeks and if I didn't like it I need not go again.

We arrived in plenty of time. I was a bit apprehensive about walking in the front door as I felt that people would be watching me and would know that I wasn't 'all there'. I went in and asked the receptionist where I needed to go.

'Go upstairs and you'll be called,' she said.

I went up and saw several small rooms leading off the waiting area. One door had a sign saying 'Susan G. Counselling In Progress' on it. I waited. I couldn't sit down as I'm a very impatient person. I can never not be doing something, so I started pacing up and down. Three forty-five and still no one had appeared. I started to think that maybe this was a sign telling me that I shouldn't be there and should just leave. I stood there with one foot pointing towards the exit door and the other facing the counsellor's door. Should I stay or should I go? I stayed and waited, mainly because I didn't want Darren, John or Vincent thinking that I was scared.

Five minutes later the door opened and I saw a distressed woman being comforted by another. I immediately put up my defensive little wall, swearing to myself that I would never cry and the counsellor would never break me. I just saw it as her versus me.

My counsellor saw the distressed lady out and asked me to come in. There were just two chairs and a coffee table in the little room. A jug of water and a box of tissues – which I decided I would never need – stood on top of the table. I sat by the window even though it was dark outside, thinking to myself that if things got too boring I could at least sit back and watch the world go by. I had kept my heavy Royal Mail coat on and soon started to feel very hot. The first thing I had to do was read through the rules, pay a voluntary contribution and sign various documents.

While reading them, I felt my counsellor looking me over, which made me very self-conscious. Since I had been made support manager I'd had to wear smart clothes, but now I looked down and remembered that the hem had come unstitched on my trousers and I hadn't bothered to sew it up. There was no way I could hide it in this small room. Despite this, after paying and signing the documents, I was keen to get on. I felt that in 12 weeks all my problems would be sorted out and I would be normal. While Susan sorted out the paperwork I had a good look at her. She seemed OK. She asked me what I expected to gain from counselling.

'I really don't know,' I answered honestly. 'Do you have a magic wand?'

'No, I'm afraid not.'

I really didn't know. I told her that I hadn't wanted to come as I wanted to face my problems and deal with them myself.

Susan seemed very nice and was about my age, which surprised me as all the other staff that I had seen there were middle-aged. She also appeared to have a strong and determined aura about her.

We settled down to business. The first session was mainly taken up with me talking about everything that had happened.

Susan would throw in the occasional: 'And how did you feel about that?'

'I don't know,' I would answer. 'I can't remember.'

She asked about my job and complimented me on how well

I'd done in such a short time. But in my view I hadn't. 'It was only because I passed the test, that's how I got it,' I told her.

'I'm sure they wouldn't have given it to you if they didn't think you were able to do it,' she said.

No, I was right. I told her that she shouldn't compliment me as I would never believe her. People only liked me for what I could do for them. All of a sudden my thoughts went back to my high-school PE teacher, who I felt didn't stick up for me because she liked me but because I was a useful player in her team.

The first session was over fairly quickly. I said goodbye and went out. As I left the waiting area another lady was entering Susan's counselling room. Bloody hell, I thought, it's like a conveyor belt, but not with nuts and bolts but with confused women.

Darren drove me home and I told him what had happened. It was easy, I felt, not at all intense. One down, 11 to go.

The following week I drove myself there, as we couldn't have Darren's dad over every week otherwise he would know something was going on. Darren had drawn me a map and I managed to get there OK. I sat in the car and looked over at the house. It made me think of Eeyore from the Winnie the Pooh stories, who always had a rain cloud hanging over him. No matter what the day was like outside, it was a house that had always seen a lot of doom and gloom. I went in and waited. This time it was just five minutes.

Susan asked how my week had been.

'Fine,' I answered. Then I asked her why she was a counsellor and how she coped with all the sadness and gloomy people that she had to deal with.

Top: Sue and her brother Paul.

Left: The family on 5 January, 1977. At the top are Anthony and Andrew, in the middle are Paul and Susan and between them is Karen.

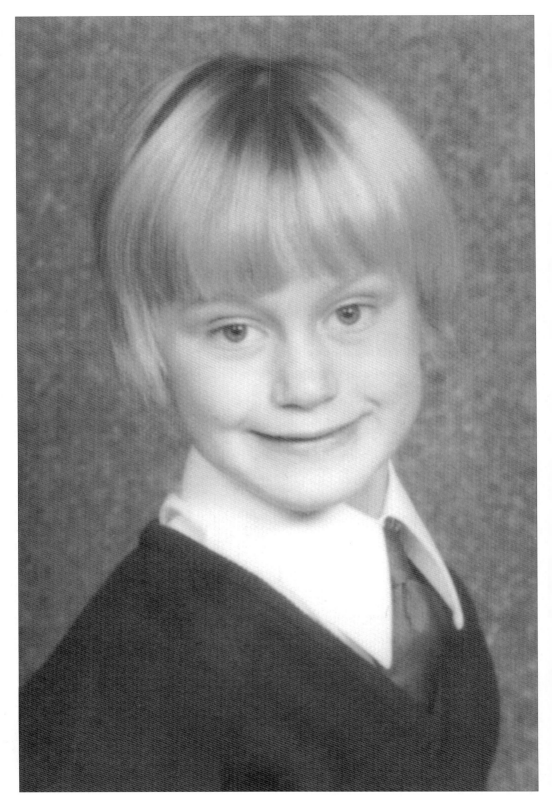

Sue aged between 5 and 6.

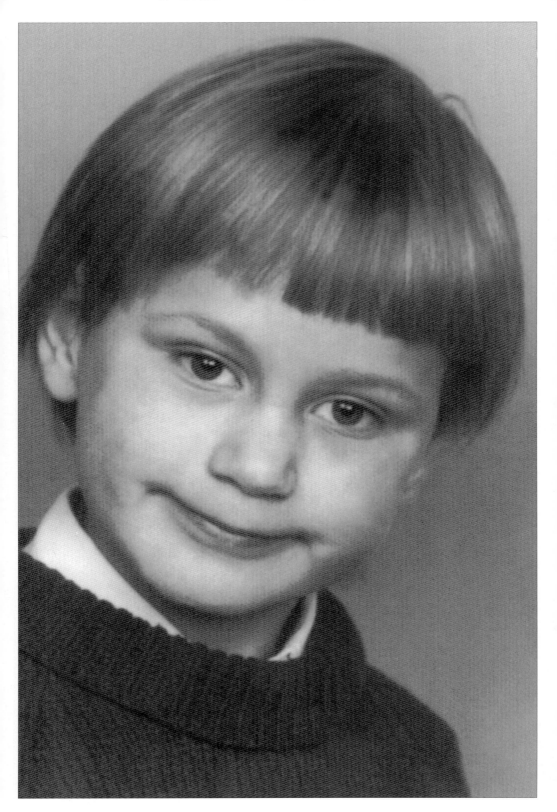

Sue aged between 7 and 8.

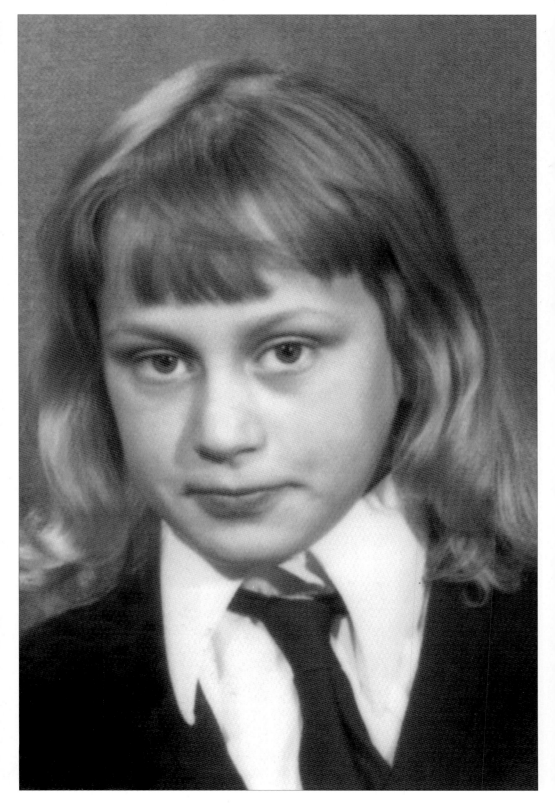

This was the photo later used in court to prove that Sue had long hair as a child.

Sue's dad at his wedding to Ela in 1996.

Sue with her children at the home-built bar in her dad's house where he used to entertain his friends.

Top: Sue with Sophie aged three and James aged two.

Bottom: Sunnier childhoods: Sue with her own kids in the summer of 1993.

Sue and her dad in the place he loved the best: his bar.

'I meet some great people,' she said. 'Like you.'

Yeah, right, I thought. I was very aware that she was watching me and probably picking up things, which I wasn't too happy about. I wasn't sure enough of her yet. I did try to hide things, but it was no good: I knew she knew. She was always saying good, positive things, but I dismissed them and assumed that she said them just because that was what she was trained to do. She asked me if I had ever enjoyed sex.

I shook my head. 'No,' I said. She asked me if I thought that my dad or stepmother had ever been abused when they were children. I automatically said no, and, even if they had been, that was no excuse. To me it's the total opposite. If they had been abused as children, that would be all the more reason not to do it to your own children. She asked how I felt about them.

'Well, I've recently been resenting my dad and have not been able to be around him. I haven't seen my stepmother for years, but I do wonder how she could, how anyone could, ever do such things to a child.' I started to think about what I'd do if I ever saw her again. Would I be able to go over to her and poke her in the eye or would the fear come back?

Susan gave me a small task to do. I was to keep a daily diary. Easy enough, I thought. After that session things started to get a lot heavier. I had lied to her already. I decided that I was going to be completely honest, otherwise there just wasn't any point in going. However, I was confused. Why did I still keep defending my dad? If I hadn't been his daughter I probably wouldn't even have liked the man. How could anyone hit a child like that? Did I push my stepmother into hitting me? Was I just a bad child that needed punishing? All of a sudden everything was beginning to weigh me down. To top it all off, my mum was coming down for a visit on my next counselling Thursday.

I filled out my daily diary and was very surprised when I read it back to myself. I had written most of it when I had been drunk and after my initial attempts to put down what was actually said I did begin to notice that I was very angry. I listened to angry music by angry people, because I seemed to identify with everything they said.

I woke up on Thursday morning with an exceptionally bad hangover. I was worried about my mum coming down. I didn't want to lose it and say something nasty (or truthful) to her and had drunk more than normal to convince myself that I wouldn't. I phoned in sick. I went to counselling and was very tense all the time. My neck kept hurting and I had to keep on rubbing it. I told Susan and she told me that it was due to stress. I smiled. Vincent had told me that once. I had rubbed my neck and he said, 'Sue, you must be stressed.' I thought he was just joking.

'Susan,' I said. 'Last week you asked if I ever enjoyed sex and I answered no. Well, that's not actually true. Sometimes when my dad was abusing me I felt moments of excitement. I don't want to lie to you. I really hate myself.'

'Most victims do,' she said, 'which is why they find it hard to tell anyone.'

I couldn't believe it! All those years I had spent stressing about it, thinking myself dirty and abnormal, only now to be told that it was a common reaction. I wasn't a freak. It was a huge load off my mind, but it didn't really sink in until a few days later, probably because I was so stressed out about my mum coming that I couldn't really think about anything else. I drove home but on the way I had to pull in to the side of the road so that I could change into my office clothes before I got back. My mum hadn't arrived yet. I told Darren about my session, even though there wasn't really much to say.

Mum came. I still had never called her that to her face. It was nice to know that she had come down to visit me. I went out to work the next morning, or rather pretended to. Instead I drove over to Karen's and spent the morning with her and Jake. I told her that my mum was down and I just couldn't handle her at the moment. She looked at me strangely but said nothing.

When Mum went home I felt relieved as now I could concentrate on my counselling. I didn't want her to know that I was in counselling, as I was sure that she would be ashamed of me and also I didn't want her to feel guilty about anything.

One night I was flicking through the TV channels when I found a programme about Fred and Rose West. Their children were giving interviews. Oh my God, I thought, now *they* really do have something to worry about. What do I have? 'Oh, my dad and stepmum were a bit nasty to me, but at least they never murdered me.' A couple of the Wests' children said, 'At the end of the day they are my mum and dad.' Yet at the time the parents were on remand for so many murders, one of them of their very own child. I just couldn't understand it.

So many flashbacks were now happening and they were really getting me down. Susan had told me to find a 'happy place' where I could relax, be calm and think about things.

At our next session I told her straight away, 'I don't have a happy place,' and said that there was always the possibility of Darren needing a hug or a kiss or, even worse, sex. Sometimes, because it had been so long, I just couldn't say no. It wasn't his fault that he was married to a freak. I just wanted so much to keep the peace. And I wanted so much for Sophie and James to have the best childhood ever. Sometimes Darren and I would watch TV in the evening and it would be some programme where a man had been cheating on his wife. Darren would turn to me and say, 'I'd never, ever do that to you.' Yet deep down I was longing for him to do just that. I was still only pretending during sex, but I wanted him to be happy. I wanted so much for him to have a proper wife.

I looked at my daughter, my beautiful daughter. I could never hit her and yet my stepmother would raise her hand as high as possible and then bring it down as hard as she could across my face. She would thump me with a fist clenched so tight that it looked like her rings were going to snap off. She would kick me, not caring what part of my body she'd got. The list is endless. How could someone do that to a small child? Was I so bad that I constantly pushed her to the limit? I began to feel that I'd made her do it.

For the next session we moved to a larger room, though it still had a coffee table with the jug of water and box of tissues on it. I noticed Susan's name on the volunteer list and asked her if she was one.

'Yes, I am. I have another job and Thursday is my day off and so I spend it here.'

Wow, she isn't even being paid to be here. My next thought

was: Why is she doing this? Am I a guinea pig? Nobody does anything for nothing. I mentioned to her that I wanted to quit the bottle. As I was still off work I thought that I might as well try it. Also, now that I knew Susan was trying to help me I felt that the least I could do was try a little to help myself. The session went OK. I didn't realise it but I was gradually telling her more and more. I was beginning to feel very guilty about the sexual abuse. 'Why didn't I just refuse to do it? They didn't force me; I just did it. Why?' I said.

Susan would reply that it wasn't my fault that these things happened and kept on telling me to look at it realistically: a full-grown man and a small child. In my mind I can't see myself and I have never been able to identify with that little girl, I told her. I didn't know whether I was cut off or just too scared to go back. I knew horrible things had happened and I knew they'd happened to me, but I still didn't see myself as that child.

She asked me to take in a photo of me as a child. I had just the one, which I hated because I've always loathed having my picture taken. It was a school photo of me with long, wavy, light-brown hair. I only kept it because it clearly showed me as having brown eyes and they had now turned green. Susan asked me to look at the photo and told me that I was a child whereas they were my parents and they set the boundaries. It was my job to do what I was told.

THIRTEEN

During the next week I kept thinking about everything. Could Susan possibly be right? She was an expert and had been a counsellor for many years, but then she didn't know me. I had some big secrets to tell her, but I wasn't ready just yet. I was also a bit scared. What if I told her and she was shocked by it? What if she said, 'Oh my God, you are a freak!' I don't know why but I felt that she must have been abused herself as a child. Maybe that's why she's in this line of work, I thought.

The next session came and Susan gave me some numbers for my local branch of AA and other support groups. I had forgotten that I had previously asked her but thanked her and took them. She said that she was unable to make the following week's session and so it would have to be cancelled. Damn it, I thought, that's one more week I'll have to wait before I become better. The session was a bit gloomy and not much happened.

I woke up the next day and rang AA. I spoke to a chap for a few minutes and he said that he would send a lady round to my house and she would come with me to a meeting. She came but I couldn't go with her. I was scared to go. What if I bump into someone that I know? I thought. Also, I am just not a group person. I always tense up and remain quiet. I adore Victoria Wood, and Darren and I went to see her on two occasions, but I couldn't relax and enjoy myself. I was sitting in the Royal Albert Hall watching a great performance but I couldn't enjoy it, as I was so aware of the people all around me. I just couldn't laugh or enjoy myself. A couple of months later, when the video came out, I would be rolling round the floor in fits of laughter, but just not in public. I thanked the AA lady for coming and told her that I couldn't do it. I had decided that I was going to do it by myself.

I told Darren that this was going to be my last boozy night. I finished all the vodka that I had, but, as it was only 9pm and this was going to be my last drinking night, I needed to make the most of it. I asked Darren to go to the off-licence, only a minute down the road, and pick me up my last-ever bottle. I think I had just two drinks out of it before I passed out on the bed. The following morning I tipped the rest of the bottle away.

I did my first day. As I was going on the wagon, I knew I would have trouble sleeping and so had decided to sleep on the sofa bed in the living room. It was also a good excuse to get away from Darren and his needs. Another good thing about my new sleeping arrangements was that I could drop off watching TV or listening to music. As I'd predicted, I did have trouble sleeping. My now sober mind was dealing with a whole new lot of childhood memories, which were rapidly appearing. I was also full of 'whys?' and 'what ifs?'. I would question everything and think over hundreds of ways that I could have done things differently. At 1am every night I would watch *The Magic Roundabout* on the cartoon channel to try to take my mind off things. But it didn't really help. When Darren and I first lived together I would put on *Mickey's Christmas Carol*, a Disney version of the Dickens classic, partly because I loved cartoons and also because I loved Christmas. I wanted to fall asleep dreaming about fun things and not about reality.

However, at that time things were much too heavy to expect a five-minute cartoon to help. I tried drinking hot milk and listening to relaxation tapes but they never worked. I was just too tense. As I was off work it didn't really matter if I couldn't sleep at night, because I had all day to catch up on any missed sleep. But the nights seemed so long.

Sometimes the mornings could be just as bad. I'd wake up with such a strong feeling of self-hate that I really didn't want to face the world and just wanted to stay in bed. No matter how much I looked at the good things in my life, sometimes I just couldn't shake off that terrible 'early morning' feeling. I now felt twice as bad, for guilt had been added to my feelings. I felt guilty about feeling sad.

One Thursday morning I was just about to have a shower and get ready for my next session. Getting ready involved being totally clean, making sure that I had proper tissues (I said that I wouldn't cry, but just in case), sunglasses (if I did cry, they would cover my tearful eyes), mints (so that I didn't smell of cigarettes) and my little squishy ball in my pocket so that I could play with it during the session. At that moment I received a phone call from the Open Door telling me that Susan had phoned in sick and was unable to attend today. I felt so let down. I really looked forward to seeing her. She is the only person that I've ever really talked to and also I was starting to believe the things she said.

At the Open Door I had seen a sign about a group that met at 11am each Friday and I decided to give it a try the day after my cancelled session. I went but hated it. I just couldn't get involved and sat quietly in a corner. Susan rang me on the Saturday. She hadn't been ill in fact but had been involved in a car crash while on her way to the Open Door. I asked if she was OK and she said yes. She asked about me. 'I'm fine,' I told her, but I was lying. I still wasn't sleeping, bad memories kept coming back, I couldn't stop crying, I couldn't figure things out in my mind, no matter how many times I thought about them, and I was worried about losing my job.

The following Thursday I went to my session and after the normal formalities Susan asked if I'd gone to AA. 'No, I just couldn't,' I said, 'so I decided to do it by myself. It'll be three weeks tomorrow.'

'What, three weeks without drinking?'

'Yes.'

'Good. I'm so proud of you. What you've done is a big thing.'

But I wouldn't let her compliment me. 'I shouldn't have got myself in that position in the first place,' I told her, but secretly I was glad that she was proud of me.

If my other problems couldn't be sorted, at least she'd had a hand in helping me give up the bottle. Over the weeks she gradually began to take away, brick by brick, my defensive little wall. She would compliment me and say nice things about me.

At first I ignored them, but, when I thought about it, Darren had said the same things, so had my friends and work colleagues. I'd got used to rubbishing it all. Darren only said it because I was his wife, and my friends to cheer me up. But why would my workmates and Susan say them? Maybe they were true. I told Susan that it was very hard when you've been brought up to think that you're shit. 'It's like being told all of a sudden that red isn't red, it's actually blue.'

'I know,' she said.

'I just want to be normal.'

'What is normal? I've never met a normal person.'

She told me that she had on her hands a six-week-old baby that had been abused by his stepfather. I couldn't believe it. A six-week-old baby? I was too scared to ask if it was sexual or physical. In my mind I was hoping that it was physical as I really couldn't imagine a man getting sexual pleasure from a baby. But it did happen and it does quite frequently. I could see an infants' school from the window of the counselling room and sometimes during my session I would see some of them leaving for home. Happy smiling children, but how many of them will be going back to an abuser? I wondered. I had been given figures but I couldn't believe it. I didn't want to believe it. I made up my mind that we live in a 'sucky' world and people were just monsters.

Susan told me about a six-year-old girl whose parents she'd met. The father had sexually abused the girl but the mother blamed her for it. 'She sexually provoked her father,' she stated. WHAT? I had to ask Susan to stop telling me these stories.

Occasionally she would throw in a question that would make

me clam up. On the other side of our wall I could hear the lady in the next room talking. I was a bit concerned that, if we could hear her, then she could hear us. Susan tried it and assured me that we had only heard the lady because she had been talking loudly over the phone. I told her that I was planning on divorcing Darren and I hated it every time that he came near me. Sometimes I would feel physically sick and most of the time it would bring back memories of my dad.

Susan gave me the name of a book and advised me to read it. *The Courage to Heal* was all about sexually abused people and what they had been through and how they were now coping with life. I found it very helpful as I knew what these women were talking about and had also experienced many of the same problems. It made me realise that the feelings that I'd been experiencing were normal. I wasn't a freak. But I still couldn't get over the hurdle that all three parents had mistreated me. Considering the injuries that I received from my stepmother, why didn't anyone else in the family do anything?

And, as much as my counsellor tried, I just couldn't get free of the idea that I was a worthless child. I began to feel that maybe counselling wasn't for me. Susan also mentioned that she hadn't been sexually abused. I didn't know why I thought she had been, but all of a sudden I felt that I couldn't now tell her my 'big secrets'. How would she know what it was like? It was a major blow, for I had been gearing myself up to telling her.

We got back on to talking about Darren and I told Susan that he could do a million good things but it would be the one tiny little thing that I would go mad over. It was like I was looking for a reason to dislike him. Although we rarely argued, when we did it was about my drinking or my selfish attitude. I couldn't believe that he could call me selfish, when everything I did was for the children, but then he didn't know, did he? Most of the time when arguments flared up I normally said nothing and just didn't speak to him for a while. I couldn't be bothered to argue and, besides, I didn't want the children to hear us and be worried. I could never keep up the silent treatment for too long, as he would make me laugh; he could always make me laugh.

'Don't notice the bad things but look at the good things,' Susan said. 'Why don't you tell him everything? I'm sure he'll understand.'

'There's absolutely no way,' I replied. 'How can I suddenly say, "Oh, hubby, by the way, I've been lying to you for the last ten years: it wasn't really good." No, I can't tell him that.' But I remembered that he had read the book and maybe he might understand. So I said I'd give it a good think.

I had started to go out for evening walks. I would put on my headphones and just wander around. I still was off work and thought that I'd better try to get back into the real world. Sophie and James were walking to and from school by themselves – although I would ring up the school secretary and ask if they'd got there OK – so, apart from the counselling, I never went out. But it had to be dark before I would go. I would walk around thinking. I was always thinking. Maybe I should tell him but what if he decided that enough was enough, living with me was too hard, and he left me? But then hadn't I wanted that anyway? Yes, but not yet. What about the children? He could fight for custody and, what with all my problems, he would probably win and then my life would be over. It was too risky telling him. But then again it's Darren, I reminded myself. He'll understand, I know he will. So I told him. He said that deep down he knew.

'We'll stop all that now and not start again until you're completely ready. Even if you're never ready, then that's OK, we'll be fine. I just want to be with you,' he said.

I burst into tears. What a guy.

I told Susan at the next session. Although things were now all out in the open, I was a little bit confused about one thing. Why, if Darren knew deep down that I wasn't enjoying it, did he still keep on trying?

I asked Susan.

'Because he loves you and that's his way of showing you. Your parents have made you all confused about love and sex, but just take things slowly and you will feel differently. It sounds like Darren is a patient man.'

By now I was regularly telling Kim and Claudette more and more about the abuse I had received. It had become easier to talk about it. I couldn't help, though, but feel that the world would be a much happier place if it weren't for sex.

Now things were a bit clearer I felt ready to return to work. Vincent, my acting manager and also my friend, came to my house to have a chat about whether I was OK to go back. A new lady had started and was to be my new manager. I told him that I would return the following week. I had taken seven weeks off work but it couldn't be helped: I had been a right mess.

Darren stopped all sexual advances, which made me more

relaxed at home. I put away the sofa bed and returned to our room. I was still on the wagon but was getting back into a routine. When Darren's arm came round me and he said, 'It's good to have you back,' I automatically held my breath, waiting, dreading the next move. But the next move never came. He had kept his word. After a while I started to relax, but not totally – just in case. Susan's words all of a sudden popped into my head: 'Look at the good things and not the bad.' I noticed how warm Darren's body was and it did feel comforting. My dad's had always been sweaty and clammy. Now why was I comparing Darren with my dad?

The following morning I returned to work. While putting on my jacket I noticed how big it was. I had lost a bit of weight during my time off and now my clothes were all too big. That's handy, I thought. Now it really looks like I've been ill and no one will ask. A lot of people came up to me and told me how good it was to see me back, which really cheered me up. I was popular at work. I would walk across the works floor and say hello to everyone. If I needed something doing, I would ask someone rather than order him or her. I always treated others just like I wanted to be treated myself. Even our customers said they had missed me, and that made me feel really good.

At my next session Susan told me that the Open Door would be closed for the next few weeks and then she would be going on holiday, so there would be no sessions for the next five weeks. I felt sad. That's another five weeks that I'll have to wait until I'm cured, I thought to myself. I still thought that at the end of the 12 weeks I would be a normal person.

Even though I was starting to trust Susan, things were going very slowly. She said that I would probably need a few extra sessions and so she booked me up for a further six, to run straight on after the 12 had finished. She said if I needed her I was to call her. I did need to phone her quite urgently. Karen had recently gone back to work and she would leave her three-year-old son, Jake, with Ela and my dad. Susan had once told me that sometimes it wasn't always about sex, but about power. It had suddenly hit me that, if he wanted to, he could mess with little Jake, my godson. I didn't want to think what he could do to him.

I was also starting to get very angry that I was going through the sleepless nights, the crying, the despair and all the stress – and not just me but Darren and the children as well – and yet my dad was living his life as normal. It just wasn't fair. He even started whining to people that I wasn't talking to him. 'I haven't done anything,' I heard him tell a niece of mine. So I started making plans. I was going to sprinkle nails down his driveway so that he would get loads of punctures. I was going to spray 'Paedophile' over his garage. I was going to let the police know that he was probably over the drink-drive limit every morning. I wanted to make sure he knew that he couldn't treat me like that and get away with it. I was really going to go ahead and do it. Sunday was Kim's birthday and she would be coming over in the evening. As it was her birthday, she'd have a glass of wine, and as I was still on the wagon I could drive her home and then put my plan into action.

On Saturday Susan rang me. I felt that she must have known what I was planning. I told her and she told me not to do it.

'But it's so unfair,' I said.

'I know. When were you planning on doing these things?'

'Tomorrow night, about midnight, after I've taken my friend home.'

'OK. I'll ring you at about 1am.'

'OK.'

I drove Kim home at 11.30, as I wanted to be back in plenty of time for Susan's phone call. I got back at 12.15 but she had already rung. Darren had spoken with her. Automatically I became very defensive. I felt that Susan had known that I wouldn't be in and intended to have a word with Darren. Once people meet or talk with him, they know what a great guy he is and it makes me feel like such a bitch for planning on leaving him. I felt that Susan would try to get bits of info out of him. Darren told me everything she had said and also that she would ring me after she'd got back from holiday.

So now I was facing a five-week break. I decided that I needed to have a chat with my brother Anthony. I rang and we arranged to meet for the day. He lived by the seaside with his partner Chris, so it would be a day out. The kids loved it at Anthony's, I think maybe because he had cats and my two loved all pets. Darren, Chris and the kids went out for a walk so that my brother and I could have a chat. I asked him if he had known that Dad abused me.

'Yes. We all knew,' he said, meaning the three oldest boys.

Once Paul had blurted out, 'Why don't you go and have sex with your daughter?' and from the way my dad reacted it was so obvious what Paul had said had some truth in it. I remembered that incident. My dad went totally crazy and really laid into Paul, and I just locked myself in my bedroom. I was

135

really shocked and embarrassed that anyone knew about it. Nothing more was ever said by anyone. Anthony told me that they had their suspicions, but after that day they all knew. He asked me a lot of questions. How old was Dad? Was he drunk? How often? Where? I gave him honest answers to everything.

It had started when I was about four years old and so Dad would have been 30. It got a lot more serious when my body started to develop, which was when I was 11 and Dad was 37. It stopped when I was about 14, maybe 15. Most of the time it happened in the evenings, when he was drunk, but there were a few times when I remembered it happening in the afternoon, when he was sober. But it seemed like it was all the time. I remember once just wishing that I could have a night off. It was nearly always downstairs in his bar-bedroom or sometimes, if Karen was away, in my room.

My nan worked for the local doctor and when he went away on holiday she would house-sit for him and sometimes take Karen and Steven along for company. Anthony felt a little indignant about my dad. He said that, when he told him that he was gay, Dad took Steven out of the bedroom and Anthony himself felt that Dad was accusing him of being a paedophile when all the time it was Dad who was the guilty one. Anthony also told me that Dad used to beat Deidre and he remembered her holding him up to defend herself against his blows. I didn't know that and started to feel a little sorry for her as I knew it wasn't nice to be beaten up.

As we talked, it began to hit me. It was my own real dad who had been doing these things. Anthony asked if Dad had had full intercourse with me. I hesitated a bit. I wanted to say no, as I had told Susan, but memories had reappeared and one of them was 'me opening my eyes and he was on top of me'. I didn't know. I felt that surely I would have known if he had but I didn't know. Maybe I was well and truly drunk, or maybe it was too painful a memory and was pushed into a dark corner of my mind with a 'Do Not Disturb' sign.

Anthony told me that he remembered an incident when my stepmother was pouring shampoo over my head and it was going into my eyes and mouth and I was screaming my head off, but she kept pouring and rubbing the shampoo in. He told me that sometimes he felt so helpless, because he wanted to help me but was too afraid of her to do anything. He also said he hadn't wanted me taken away to 'the home'. After our talk he gave me a hug, told me that he loved me and wished me luck.

My next task was to tell Karen. I decided that, if I were her, I would want to know. She knew that I was in counselling but thought it was because of my stepmother's treatment, which at first it was. I rang her on a Sunday afternoon; she was decorating and I asked if I could pop over and see her. I also checked if her boyfriend was there as I felt that she might be shocked about what I was going to tell her and I wanted her to have some support. When I got there little Jake's face appeared at the window. He looked excited because we always had fun playing. Karen and I went into the garden. She was very nervous and kept asking if I was OK. I think she thought that I was going to tell her that I was really ill.

'Karen, I'm telling you this because I feel you have a right to know. The last few weeks Darren and I have been torn about telling you but, because of Jake, I've got to. Between the ages of four and fourteen Dad sexually abused me. I always believed that it was my fault but now I know it wasn't.'

As soon as I said it, I knew that it really wasn't. I had a photo of me, taken when I was seven and I would sometimes look at it. I pictured me, this little girl, being beaten up by one parent and then running to the other for love but only getting a cuddle if I did 'something nice'. I now remembered that even when I had done 'something nice' my dad would leave or tell me to go. And I didn't remember ever getting my cuddle. I didn't tell Karen this. She cried, gave me a hug and said she was sad and sorry for me.

'Don't worry about me. I'm getting it sorted,' I told her. 'I had to tell you because of little Jake.'

Even though my dad is so anti-gay, I had to explain to Karen that sexual abuse wasn't always about sex but sometimes to do with having power over another, weaker person. She said that she would know if anything had happened to Jake. I had noticed during my chats with Anthony and Karen that while I was explaining things to them I was actually starting to believe them myself.

It was a very stressful time for me. Darren came up with the idea of cashing in his insurance policies and going on a holiday of a lifetime. He met me at work one lunchtime and we had a look in the travel agents. Disneyworld, Florida: could there be any other holiday of a lifetime? We both felt the same, and booked for two weeks for the following Easter. It was just under a year away but it was a damn good thing to look forward to.

I had now settled back into work. My new boss was OK. I hadn't been looking forward to working with another woman, especially as she was a lot younger than me. I'd been wondering what we'd have to talk about but we got on really well and made each other laugh. Surprisingly, she managed to put up with my strops, which would still flare up all of a sudden. Something would enter my mind and, no matter how much I tried to work it out, I could never find the answer. It would make me annoyed because I hate not knowing. She knew something was up with me; she never asked but she did say that if I ever needed anything I should let her know.

One evening I rang my old college friend Wendy.

'Hiya, Wendy. How are you? I tried ringing you a few days ago but you were away. Where you been – anywhere nice?'

'Hi, Sue. I'm fine. I was actually in court,' she replied.

'Why, what've you done?' I asked jokingly.

'I've done nothing,' she said. She then started telling me about her scout leader, who had abused her and several other girls during her teens. One of them had reported him to the police and they asked Wendy to be a witness and give evidence in court.

'Oh my God,' I said. 'All this time we've been friends and I didn't know.'

'No, nobody knew. Not even my parents,' she said.

I started to tell her about my dad and stepmum and what I was going through at the moment, just to let her know that I could identify a little with her. She was as astounded as I had been by her story.

I had now been on the wagon for ten weeks and had made up my mind that I would also pack up smoking – again. As it was a bank holiday on the Monday I decided that Sunday was a good day to stop, because then I would have two non-smoking days before I returned to work. I had been on 20 a day for years but was always ashamed of it. I would never smoke in public or in front of others. Since I had been back at work I noticed others' smoky breath and smelly, sweaty bodies. I was very paranoid about being smelly, so I would always have with me a box of Smints for my breath and an Impulse deodorant spray.

I got up late on Sunday, after staying up late and making the most of smoking my last cigarettes. I lasted two hours – that was it. I had to go and buy a packet. I felt such a failure that I bought a bottle of drink as well. The next day I was so ill, after being sick all night. I also felt unbelievably worthless as this time yesterday I had been a non-drinker and a would-be non-smoker. I decided to put the drinking down to 'one night of madness' and stay off it. It was an easy decision, for I felt so ill. I hadn't had hangovers for years but maybe over the past ten weeks my body had got used to being alcohol-free and rebelled.

FOURTEEN

My return to counselling was fast approaching and I was sort of expecting Susan to ring me, even if only to see how I was. She had told Darren that she would call but she never did. The Thursday came and I went along, although this time I wasn't as keen as normal. I asked if she'd had a good holiday and then immediately tore into her.

'Why didn't you ring me?' I asked. I felt hurt that she hadn't as I thought that she knew me by now and would know that I wouldn't say something and not do it. Also, for a solitary person like me, a phone call is a big thing; it's a connection to the outside world. She said, sorry, she had meant to call but she had been busy. Straight away my thoughts went back to seeing her name on the volunteer list and I realised she didn't have to be there at all, so I should be grateful for what time she did give me. To complicate things, Darren and I had previously discovered that one of our health insurances covered us for counselling costs. I should really have quit then, but I didn't want to as I felt that I had come so far that I didn't want to start all over again with someone else on a fee-paying basis. Susan had done so much for me in the few weeks that I had known her and I really did want to trust her. I told her all about my chats with my brother and sister and also about my recent night of drinking. She asked how I felt about this.

'I just had a night off,' I said. 'I can't let it ruin the last ten weeks, otherwise I will get depressed. I'll just carry on. It's like riding a bike: you fall off, then you get straight back on.' I told her about Anthony and all the things he told me. Then I told her about Karen and also Wendy. There was a lot of bad news to be told in that session.

As soon as I left the session I felt like a right spoiled brat. After all she had done for me, I went crazy about a silly little phone call.

The night before my next session I couldn't sleep. I was tossing and turning for hours and then suddenly, at about 4am, I decided that I did trust Susan and was going to tell her some of my big secrets. The next day I entered her room and immediately apologised for my behaviour. I told her that I did trust her and that I would tell her one of the things that had been bothering me for years.

'But I can't tell you until five minutes before the end. I need to tell you and then go,' I said. I thought that this was the best way as then she could have time to think about things and not accidentally blurt out, 'Oh my God, Sue, you are a slut.' Not that she would have done – I knew that – but I just wanted to tell her and get out of there.

'OK, Susan,' she said – I'd never told her that I preferred to be called Sue – 'we have five minutes left now.'

As I stood up I asked her not to look at me. Then, after an immense amount of stammering and stuttering, I blurted out, 'When I was 11 years old I asked my dad what oral sex was and he showed me. I can't remember what I exactly said but I was 11 years old and had literally asked to go down on my dad. Goodbye.'

I flew out of that room and left the building. I had to take a few minutes before I started the car, just to catch my breath. I remember the incident so clearly. I had been reading *Summer Term at St Clare's*, in which one of the girls, Bobby, changed the clock so that they didn't have time to do an oral maths test. I assumed oral meant talking about it. I soon realised that it wasn't and I always remember thinking to myself that I would never ask a question again, ever. The following week I felt so bad. The lowest ever. I had to go to counselling on the Thursday, but for the first time I really didn't want to go. I was embarrassed about facing Susan. Besides, I still felt that I should give up my place to someone else as I had insurance cover to go elsewhere. Again, I got very drunk on the Wednesday night.

The following day I walked into the room but wouldn't look at Susan. I told her that I felt so ill. Darren had to take me in that day, as I was too hungover to drive. I was close to throwing up. I always took along my own bottle of water, but it had run out after about five minutes and I asked if the water in the jug was tap water.

'Yes, it is, but here, have some of mine,' Susan said and she poured some into my bottle.

'What about my revelation last week?' I asked.

'OK. You were 11, a child. If you went in and straddled him it wouldn't matter. It doesn't mean that you are asking for it. He, as an adult, should not have done it.'

'Have you ever heard of anything so bad?' I asked.

'Oh much, much worse,' she answered.

That was a load off my mind. I wasn't the worst person in the world. I started to totally confide in Susan. I told her that my dad would buy me presents after the incidents and, though I really enjoyed having the gifts back then, now I felt really guilty about it.

'Well, that's only natural,' she said. 'Who doesn't enjoy receiving presents?'

'But I yelled at him to stop and he did. Why didn't I yell at him before? Why did I keep doing the "things"? He never threatened me or beat me.'

Susan explained to me that my father had brought me up to do these things and not think twice about them, but I obviously reached the age when I realised that it was wrong.

I then told her that I behaved really badly at school and my dad was often called in to see the headmistress. He would always forgive me after I'd done 'something' for him.

'Why didn't I just behave at school and then I wouldn't have had to do it on those occasions?' I asked. But I would never have been a good school child. I swore to myself after my stepmother had gone that I was going to do what I liked when I liked and with whom I liked. I had freedom.

'He used the excuse, not you. If it wasn't school behaviour, he would have found something else,' Susan replied. 'It's the same as your stepmother. No matter what you'd done, there was always going to be something she'd get you for. When there wasn't anything, then she'd invent something.'

I told her that I felt that I was a useless wife and mother. I sometimes wished that Darren would dump me and find himself a nice wife and she would be a better mum to my kids than I ever could be. But I couldn't have that. There is no way that I would allow another woman to be a mother to my kids, but then what if it was better for the children? I love my children to bits and would do anything for them, but how could I teach my little girl to be a woman when I didn't know myself?

I felt very depressed as I told Susan this.

'What do you think being a woman means?' she asked.

'Well, teaching her about clothes, make-up, jewellery, men.' This was the closest that I ever came to crying. Tears were starting at the corners of my eyes, and I just about managed to keep them in.

'But that's not what is important,' Susan answered.

Sophie was a fan of Steps and so for her birthday we bought her tickets to their concert. The show was coming closer and she was getting very excited. The day arrived, and Darren was going to drop Sophie and me off at Wembley Arena and pick us up afterwards. Sophie was a very excited ten-year-old. She had a great time and squeezed my hand and said, 'Thanks, Mum.' That's what being a mum is all about. It had been a terrific evening, although having thousands of kids screaming or blowing into their whistles had probably damaged my hearing. Still, it was good to know that all those children were having a wonderful time.

Darren and I had restarted our physical relationship, although I did have a list of definite 'don'ts'. We started off very slowly and Darren even said that if I wanted to stop at any time I should just tell him and he would stop. Things were going OK. I was now at the stage where I was starting to semi-enjoy things. A few months previously, after sex was finished I would immediately pull the duvet over me, get a nightshirt on and rush into the bathroom to have a shower. If I had felt any enjoyment at all, a tidal wave of disgust would sweep over me. Now I was starting to become more relaxed. Sometimes I had images of my father, and normally they would appear right at the moment when I didn't want them to. But then sometimes I didn't. Darren broke my rules by doing something that was on my 'Do not do' list one night. I don't know if he forgot or just got caught up in the moment.

I went to counselling the next day and told Susan about the concert. She would always tell me that I was a strong person but I never believed her.

'Look at what you've done for your children. So many others can't do it, but you can.'

Maybe she's right, I thought to myself.

When I got home Sophie had a friend in and was showing her all her Steps goodies she had bought the previous night. I heard her friend say, 'You're so lucky, Sophie. I wish I had a mum like yours.'

OK, Susan was right. It made me realise that I wasn't a useless waste of space and things were going to get better. No more sitting back and taking it. Later I told Darren that he had broken the rules and he apologised and said that he didn't know that he had but would be more careful in the future.

My counselling sessions were soon coming to an end, which I felt was a great pity as I did enjoy chatting to Susan. The sessions always flew by and sometimes I was quite surprised when she said, 'Time's up.' It felt like I'd just sat down. I had never told a soul any of my deepest thoughts and now I realised that I had told Susan, Darren, Anthony, Karen, my friend Wendy, Vincent and a few other friends from work. My workmates were absolutely dumbfounded by the news. They all said much the same thing: 'We always thought that you were so happy and content with life, as you always have a smile on your face.'

It was true. I would spend my day being happy but I was covering up the fact that I was very sad and scared. I was pretending.

Susan's remarks over the past few months had gradually sunk in.

We were now on our seventeenth session. The following week's was cancelled but there would be one the week after: our last. I told Susan that I had been out with Ela the previous weekend and she'd kept praising my dad and saying what a great man he was. I told Susan that if I were Ela I would want to know exactly what sort of man I'd married. She mentioned that one of her other ladies had pressed charges against her abuser and was now in prison. I couldn't believe that she had been believed. I told Susan that I was now ready to confront my dad.

'Put something between you, a table or a chair – anything,' she warned me.

'I'll be fine,' I said.

It was my birthday on the Saturday and Ela brought my card round. Only she had signed it: my dad's name was blatantly left off. She asked me where I kept disappearing to every Thursday.

If only she knew, I thought.

The following Thursday Darren and I went to see a solicitor. I wanted to get legal advice before doing anything else. I had a list of questions. How much will it cost? Can I be sued if my dad is found not guilty? How long will it take? Will I have to go to court? And, finally, will I be believed as it's now 20 years later? I told the solicitor and she picked up the phone and asked the police what I should do next.

'Finish the counselling and then call this number and we'll arrange to meet,' said the police officer.

The solicitor told me that I wouldn't have any costs. I was to report to the police and, if the Crown Prosecution Service (CPS) thought that there was a case, they would go ahead and press charges. All we were doing was reporting a crime to the police.

It felt good. All of a sudden I had all this power. For a moment I had every intention of going round to my dad's and telling him that I could have him arrested if I wanted to. I thought about it and realised that if I were faced with prison I would do anything possible to avoid it. I felt that my dad might say sorry but he wouldn't really mean it: he'd just say it in the hope of shutting me up. I was sure that, deep down, he'd probably think that I wouldn't go through with it. I imagined him all sad, asking everyone, 'Why is she doing this to me?' My eyes were now wide open. I could see that to my dad nothing he had ever done was his fault.

I rang Anthony and told him that I was thinking about reporting both my parents to the police. I asked how he felt about it. He told me that he'd already had a word with his counsellor friend about the same thing and she had asked him, 'How would it affect your relationship with your father?'

He replied, 'I don't really have a relationship with him. He never calls or visits.'

Anthony told me that he loved me and was there for me. I asked him how Chris, his partner, felt about it. He told me that Chris had advised him not to get involved. Anthony told me that we were all involved, because it had happened and shouldn't have done. It was a horrible way to grow up.

Little Sara Payne had gone missing. I was in the smoke room at work when the newsreader on the radio said she still hadn't been found. There were a couple of young lads there with me. I never really spoke to them as they worked in a different department. Both were in their early twenties: young, carefree guys. 'Poor little mite. She's probably dead by now,' one of them said.

'A pity we can't get our hands on the bastard that did it,' said the other one, a huge skinhead. 'I'd give him a lesson he'd never forget.'

'Yeah. And make sure you had your Totecs on while giving it to him,' said another guy. While working on the Ops floor we all had to wear these protective shoes with a steel toecap.

These guys were young and they weren't fathers, yet they knew just how unacceptable some things are. Child abuse, especially sexual abuse, is wrong.

All week I thought non-stop about everyone in the family. Aunts, nephews, nieces, everyone. I knew it would affect them all. All the adults would have to live with it. I couldn't risk another little girl being abused by him. And I wanted my justice. I had to report him. What if he'd done it before? If he had and it had been reported, I might not have had to go through it. But what if I didn't report him and he did it again? No. I had no choice: I had to report him. I also strongly believe that child abuse is wrong. I can't say it's wrong and express my disgust at all child abusers while all the time turning a blind eye to my abusers just because they're my parents.

My last counselling session was approaching. I had noticed during my time there that the walls were a bit bare and so I bought two dolphin posters and had them framed. I was very embarrassed about taking them in. I was originally going to pay the postage and send them but I didn't want them to get broken.

Susan called me in.

'Hang on a sec,' I said, and she came over to me. 'I just thought that these might cheer up the walls a bit.' She was well chuffed and called out to her supervisor. I immediately became very embarrassed. There they were thanking me when really it should have been me thanking them. I think they knew that this was my way of saying thanks.

The last session was a little subdued. I told Susan about my meeting with the solicitor and she asked me what I was going to do.

'I don't know,' I answered. 'But I can't help thinking that, if it was my husband, father, grandfather, whatever, then I would want to know.'

I worried that, because he had got away with doing it to me, he might now see it as acceptable behaviour. I didn't think that he would mess around with another little girl but what worried me were the 'innocent' accidents – 'Oh, sorry, I didn't know you were having a bath' – that meant he could get an eyeful. This he could easily do. All of a sudden memories came flooding back. Whenever Karen had friends over I would be there. If my friends invited me for a sleepover I wouldn't go, but they could come to my place. He had never tried it on with another child, I thought, but then how did I know that? I didn't.

Susan and I said goodbye. She said she wanted to give me a hug but knew that I wasn't the huggy type. I thanked her most sincerely and left. I knew that I would see her again. I'd had my suspicions that she'd been using a gym near my home. Several weeks earlier I had spotted her there, but decided that I was just seeing things. One day I noticed her car parked outside the gym, so I knew that it was definitely her. I just had this feeling that it wasn't goodbye for ever.

As soon as I got home I rang the local police station, but there was no answer and so I left a message. I rang them again in the morning and arranged to meet a woman police constable there the very next day.

FIFTEEN

Darren and I met the PC at the police station on Friday, 28 July 2000 at midday. She asked how I was and told me that she had received my telephone message but had been unable to call me back about it as she didn't know if I was a child or an adult. For this reason we had to have a face-to-face meeting. I told her that my parents had abused me when I was a child. I basically gave her a mini-rundown of my life. She did get confused about my family and all the brothers and sisters that I had, and so a rough family tree was drawn. I asked her what would happen now that I had reported my parents.

'Firstly, I will need to come and get your statement and also statements from anyone else that can help. I then present all the information to my superior and he will decide whether we have enough to bring them in for questioning. If so, we'll arrest them, question them and get their statements. This all then goes to the CPS, who will then go through everything and decide what, if any, charges can be made. If charges are made, it then goes to court,' the PC explained.

It all sounded so heavy. I also began to realise that quite a few people were going to have to believe me. If they didn't, it was all over.

The officer arranged an appointment for the following Tuesday and Wednesday, when she would come to my flat and take my statement. I thought that it would be a good idea if I wrote down my memories. I told my boss, Kathy, about the things that were happening, although I didn't go into great detail. I told her that I didn't need Thursdays off any more but I did need to take Tuesday and Wednesday off the following week and asked if I could book them as holiday.

'No. You can have them as paid special leave,' she said. Kathy was great about everything. She knew that I was battling against my parents but she never asked questions, which I was thankful for. If I wanted to tell her, then I would do, but I had only known her for a short while.

Tuesday came. I had been thinking about what I was going to tell the policewoman, and so that I didn't forget I wrote down a short list. Darren took the kids out to Richmond for the day. She arrived. I was very nervous. Once today was over with, there would be no going back. I started to tell her, and began with my dad's abuse. I told her about the gifts that he would buy me after incidents. One was Abba's album *Voulez Vous*. I even remembered the price: £5.49. I told her that I would get into trouble at school and he would forgive me if I 'did things' for him. I told her about the time when I was four and my dad told me that there were a hundred thousand babies in his hankie, which he had just put the white stuff into. I remembered looking and thinking, Where? I was going to the Isle of Wight and was about to have a bath when he appeared and gave me £3 spending money. It was the afternoon and he wasn't drunk. My dad insisted that he wasn't an alcoholic as he never drank during the day, only in the evenings. I even told her about the time in netball when I couldn't jump for fear of everyone seeing the red sores that his unshaven chin had caused.

The policewoman was scribbling away.

'Is your hand hurting?' I asked her.

'No, I'm used to it,' she replied. 'But we'll have to stop for lunch soon. I'll go back to the office and see you at two.'

'Yeah, that's fine,' I answered.

I had thought long and hard about what I was going to say about my stepmother.

We started again after lunch. I told her about the *Paddington Bear* incident and getting caught when I left my bedroom and then having talc sprinkled on the floor outside my door. There was the incident when she smashed my head into the sink. And at the kitchen table, when she held a knife to my throat. That was the first time I thought I was going to die, I told her. She ripped or broke a lot of my things, I said. Then there was the Christmas when she took all presents away from me. The night when she taped me. The *Top of the Pops* incident; I could still remember crawling up the stairs in pain. I had to get up those stairs quickly, before she returned, but I just couldn't move very quickly. The fingernail punishment. The fact that most of the time I wasn't allowed to eat with them, and when I did I had some very strict table rules to abide by. Her nickname for me: shitface. All this I said in a very shaky voice.

'Do you need to rest your hand yet?' I asked the PC.

'No, we're nearly done now.'

'What's going to happen now?'

'I'll come back tomorrow with the statement paper and rewrite everything. You'll have to read it and sign it. It will be pretty much a very boring day for you, but it needs to done.'

'OK, just one more thing. I am not going to pull out. I will see this through to the end,' I told her. I had been very shaky and close to tears a few times and thought that she may have been thinking that I'd be too scared to go through with it.

'OK. Before I go I need to know who else knows, and when they knew, as I will need statements off them,' she said.

'Kim, Claudette and Mary [my brother Andrew's first wife] have all known for some time and my brother Anthony just recently, although he already knew about my stepmother's physical abuse as he witnessed some of it.'

Our talk ended and the policewoman returned the next day with her statement paper. She had been right: it was a very boring day for me, but I had to hang around because occasionally she needed to ask me something. I spent most of the day smoking in the kitchen, probably not just out of boredom but also because I was a little nervous. This was it now: it really had become official. At last the statement was done. I had to read through it and if there was any wrong information it had to be corrected. I then signed every page – there were over 50 of them – and every correction.

While reading what I'd said I became very angry. Seeing it in black and white made it seem so real. It also made me feel very sad again for that little girl that no one cared a toss about. I gave the PC a copy of my birth certificate, the statutory declaration of my change of name from Jennifer to Susan and school reports. She was a little concerned that my birth hadn't been registered until I was two years old, and asked if I knew why. I had asked my real mum but she had said that she had never done one for me. In her first letter to me she did say that she had just assumed that my dad and stepmother had passed me off as one of their own children.

My dad had said that he had never done one either. If he had, he would have put me down as Susan Hamford and not Jennifer Doonie. He said that back in those days there were roaming registrars who went round to the hospitals and filled out birth certificates on the spot. Maybe they had got my mum to do one and she hadn't been aware of it. I still don't know.

Anthony, Claudette and Kim were next to make their statements. It was decided that Mary would have to wait until after the arrests had been made. Anthony and I were still in frequent contact. He had told me that his evidence might not be useful as he had been a child at the time and things seem more scary when you're younger. He also told me that he wouldn't say anything against Dad. He was very concerned about me, but I told him that I was fine. I explained that I had to do it and he understood. He knew what it was like growing up in our home.

Now she had got all the statements, the PC needed to speak to my mum. I wasn't very happy about it, as I didn't really want her involved. I never wanted her to regret allowing me back into her life. The police officer made arrangements to meet her but cancelled at the last minute. I was very thankful about that. The only thing I could now do was wait. We needed the officer's superior to give the green light. It was my dad's birthday in September. I did hope that he wouldn't be arrested around then. He wasn't, but I didn't go round to his place or send him a card. I had never missed my dad's birthday before.

The policewoman rang me. 'I've been told to pull them in for questioning. I'll be speaking to your dad on Monday and then your stepmother on Tuesday.'

'OK. Thanks for letting me know.'

I felt that I had won the first battle and was very relieved. I hadn't really thought about what I'd do if the police decided not to press charges.

In the event, the arrests had to be cancelled because the public were rebelling against the soaring price of petrol and the country was at a near standstill. To save petrol, the police officer could use her car only for emergencies.

I had become very nervous. It had hit me that this was really serious and there was now no way back. I saw my dad on the Monday. I often saw him driving about but I always looked the other way. All of a sudden a surge of power swept over me. He was living his life as normal but I knew that it was all about to come crashing down. I remembered telling Susan, my counsellor, how unfair it was, but now things were starting to balance out. The saying 'the past has a way of catching up with you' sprang to mind. I was no longer the confused and frightened little girl. My eyes were now fully open as to what sort of people the two of them were and I wanted them to know that they shouldn't have treated me like that. They were wrong and I was not prepared to sit back and let them get away with it. But it wasn't done purely for revenge or out of my own personal sense of justice. It felt more like: 'This is yours – take it back.'

One Monday afternoon while I was at work I received a phone call from the police officer. Earlier that morning she had arrested my dad and he had denied everything. She had questioned him and taken a mugshot, fingerprints and a DNA sample. She told me that she turned up in the police van and took him in. I know that it's going to sound mean but I couldn't help but feel secretly pleased. Imagine his shame at being taken away in front of the whole neighbourhood. He'd now have the worry, like I had for many years, about everyone finding out. I imagined him sitting in the police cell. He wouldn't have sat there and regretted abusing me, but would just be wishing that I'd kept my mouth shut.

That evening I phoned Anthony. He told me that Dad had rung everyone and told them what I'd done. Very clever of him to get the first word in. Steven was absolutely distraught and so Anthony had to come down to console him. He asked Anthony if it was true. Anthony said that he didn't know. I was a bit upset by this. Anthony did know. Why didn't he tell Steven the truth? After a while I decided that maybe Steven was too distraught and couldn't handle the complete truth. I was very worried about Karen, but I decided that I would wait for her to call me. I was sort of expecting some members of the family to ring to see if I was OK, but no one did.

My stepmother was to be pulled in the next day. I anxiously waited for the phone call confirming it but it never came. I rang the PC, who told me that they had gone round to her house but she wasn't in and so they were going back tomorrow. Tomorrow came and again no phone call. I called the PC and was told that my stepmother had been out, but a note had been left asking her to call the PC. My stepmother called the policewoman that very afternoon. It was arranged that she would go to the police station and meet her the next day at 11am.

That was the exact time that I had arranged to meet my old counsellor, Susan. I was disappointed to have to cancel but I needed to stay by the phone. I rang Susan and told her I was OK. She knew that I wouldn't cancel unless I had to. Again I anxiously waited by the phone. I rang the PC in the end. Yes, my stepmother had been in and questioned. I have to admit that I did secretly feel victorious. Just imagine how she felt. She now knew that I was grown up and kicking ass. It was 21 years since she had left and I bet she hadn't given another thought to the way she treated me. Now she had to. The PC told me that she'd asked her if she was aware that my father had also abused me. She had replied no and the PC told me that she seemed quite shocked by this. 'Pot', 'kettle' and 'black' were the words that immediately sprang to mind. Now she had to go home and tell her husband and kids what was happening. I'm sure both my father and my stepmother had many a sleepless night worrying about what could happen.

They were both told to report to the police station the following month and also not to contact me or anyone else who had made a statement. Mary could now give her statement. I had got drunk one night a few years back and told her on the phone what my dad had done. She also knew a bit about my stepmother's abusive behaviour as she had been married to my brother Andrew and he had probably told her things.

Now all we could do was wait. The CPS would be given all the evidence and they would decide if a prosecution was to be brought.

Karen rang me on the Saturday. As soon as I heard her voice I yelled to the family, 'It's Karen. Yeah.' We were all very pleased and I told her that.

'I'm going to say the same to you as I said to Dad,' she said. 'I do not want to get involved, so don't ever put me in the middle.'

'That's fine,' I said. I was so glad that she had rung. It had been a long week not knowing whether she would call or not.

The six weeks were nearly up and so I rang the PC. She told me that the CPS hadn't got back to her and so another six weeks would be needed. At first I was a little cheesed off as I wanted to know whether or not charges would be made. But then I realised that, if the CPS had said, 'No, we'll have to let it go', it would have been all over. If it sounds mean, well, I don't care, but I was thinking that now at least the two of them would have another six weeks to worry about it. I'd had years worrying about it; an extra six weeks was nothing.

Christmas came and went and we had a good time. This was the first Christmas that I had spent without visiting the Hamford family. I did miss them, especially Ela. Of all my 'mothers' she was definitely the kindest and I loved her to bits. We still visited Darren's family. They were a little curious as to why I had ceased contact with my family but realised something heavy was up and so never asked any awkward questions.

Darren's dad had just recently packed up smoking after being a 20-a-day man for nearly 40 years. I decided that, if he could do it, so could I. This was definitely it, and on 28 December I stopped smoking.

It was Jake's birthday in January. Karen did a little party and we went. Once everyone had left, Karen and I began to chat. She started telling me about her Australian cousin, Kirsty, coming over for a visit. At first she was meant to stay with her aunt, my stepmother Deidre, but my stepmother had said no and so Karen told Kirsty that she could stay at Dad's house. I didn't say anything at the time but when I got home I rang Karen and asked her why she was sending people round there while all this police business was going on. I asked her if she believed me about the abuse.

'It's not that I don't believe you, it's just that I don't want to,' she replied.

'But, Karen, there is a good possibility that he might go to prison and you're sending family, especially his ex-wife's relations, round there. Don't you think it might be a little awkward for them? Why do you think Deidre, their aunt, turned them down? It's not going to go away, it's happening and you're going to have to realise it. I don't understand why you're carrying on as if nothing has happened.'

Deep down it really hurt me. I love my little sister so much. Every single time she'd been in trouble, I'd always been there for her. When Karen was bullied at school, I went down there. I saw her in tears and went storming off to the classroom to find the little bitch who had dared to hurt my little sister. The secretary calmed me down and assured me that the headmaster would sort it out.

One night Karen ate an ice cream and it contained nuts, but we didn't know at the time that she was allergic to them. I got the phone call and went rushing over to the hospital but my dad didn't even pick up the phone to ask how she was. Ela asked, which was nice, but I know Karen would have liked her own father to have shown her a little concern. When Karen found out she was pregnant she was petrified, just like I was. I was there for her then, and she knew I would always be there for her. We were both very tearful now.

'Karen, please. I don't want to live my life not knowing little Jake.'

'And I can't live without Sophie and James.'

'Then just think about it and let me know.'

I never heard from Karen again. She worked in a supermarket right over the road from me and one day I saw her and she gave me such a defiant look. It seemed to say: 'Well, you gave me the choice and I didn't choose you.'

But that wasn't what I meant. I just wanted her to know what was going on. I was shocked and couldn't believe that Karen could give me such a horrible look. I never believed that she would turn against me.

It was James's birthday on Sunday and she never rang him or sent him a card. So now I knew we had lost Karen. We did bump into her a few times but she looked the other way, which upset me. Darren and I talked about the possibility of moving away.

I bumped into Susan, my old counsellor, one Sunday morning. She asked how things were going.

'We're still waiting for the CPS,' I told her.

'What's up?' she asked. She didn't really need to have counselling skills to notice how depressed I was.

'My sister's not talking to me,' I told her. 'She gave me such a look that it really hurt me. For a start, I didn't think my sister could do such a thing and secondly I never thought she would do it to me.'

'Maybe all she needs is time.'

'Maybe,' I said, but deep down I knew that it wasn't so. 'Anyway, we're thinking about moving. I really do need to get away from here.'

'Good idea. Fresh start.'

We chatted for a few minutes about her family and then said goodbye. It had been good to see her again.

Darren and I decided that we were serious about moving. I had never liked living in our flat as it was situated on a main road and I always felt that I, and even more my children, were being watched. There were so many flats opposite, either side of us and overlooking our back garden. We heard of a scheme that was being run by a housing association. They would help us buy a home anywhere in the country and would put up 25 per cent of the price. It was a great idea and so we made an appointment with them. We saw a lady who checked our employment details and said we could go ahead and find a property and, yes, they would buy 25 per cent of the house. There were a few conditions. We had to pay for a top-quality survey, we had to pay all the legal costs and stamp duty and when we sold the house we would have to give them back 25 per cent of the house's current value. It all seemed fair enough.

A mortgage adviser came round and told us how much we could borrow, and so all we needed to do now was find a property. We didn't really know where to start looking and so we drove up the M40 – we both needed to be near it for access to our jobs – and picked out towns along the way. We found a lovely house just over 50 miles away. We put in an offer and we got it. Now all we had to do was to sort out the mortgage and the legal stuff.

Then I heard the news that the CPS had spoken to my PC, and both my parents had eight charges against them. She explained that it wasn't a matter of eight separate incidents but, particularly in my stepmother's case, each charge covering maybe two or three incidents. Now I really was scared. I was going to have to stand up in court. The possibility had always been there, but now it was real; it was definitely going to happen.

SIXTEEN

Our next big event was our family holiday in Florida. None of us had ever flown before and we were all very excited about this completely new experience. I tried very hard to enjoy the holiday, but the court cases were always hanging over me. We had a great time, though – the rides and some of the shows at Disneyworld were brilliant – and it's a holiday we'll always remember.

When we arrived back home we found out that we could move into our new house in six weeks' time, on 4 June, and we started packing. The PC told me that my dad's case would be first and my stepmother's would be straight after, and each would probably last two to three days. The starting date was 16 July, one day after my birthday, although that wasn't definite as both cases had been put into the 'warned list'. This meant that when a courtroom became available we would be squeezed in. Strange system, I thought to myself.

My niece Hallie, Mary's daughter, had left her mum to go and live with her father, my brother Andrew. Hallie went back to her mum and told her that Andrew was going to run me over with his lorry. I was at work when I got the call. I started to shake and fear swept over me. I was sent home. Kathy told me not to come back the next day either, and not to worry as I could make the time up later. I was scared. Was this what my life was now going to be about? Would I spend the rest of it always looking over my shoulder? Would my brothers come and find me? What about my stepmother's children? I knew she had two boys who were in their late teens or early twenties. What if they were the sort of people who would track me down and give me a good hiding? What if they couldn't get to me? Would they then try to get my children? I was having all sorts of nightmares. I was now half-regretting starting court procedure. What if I've put my children in danger? I thought. I couldn't wait to move out of London.

I found some large boxes at work and Kim's dad, David, came and picked them up to deliver them to my flat. We got chatting. He mentioned prisoners and how they used to sew mailbags.

'That could be my dad in a few months' time,' I told him.

'What?' he asked, so I told him.

'Christ,' he said. He was very shocked and upset. 'I hated even having to tell Kim off. I can't imagine how a man could do that. Good on you, Sue.'

I felt good. Every person that I had told had said that I was doing the right thing. I was, however, very uncertain about whether or not I had made the right move. But the more support people showed for what I was doing, the better I felt.

We moved on 4 June, as planned. I was so glad. Everyone who was told our new address was sworn to secrecy. This was going to be a new start for my family. Luckily, Darren got a transfer to our local office, but I still had to travel into Greenford each day. I had put in for a transfer but there wasn't much hope of getting one as vacancies were just not appearing. It was great living in our new town. I could walk around and not be afraid of bumping into anyone I knew.

But I hated driving into London every day. As soon as I got halfway there my stomach would start to get all knotty and I would feel gloomy. Coming home was a different matter. Halfway down the motorway the road cuts through a hill and as you come out the other side all you see is lovely countryside. This was now my home and I loved it. All I had to do was get the court cases over and done with and then I could start to enjoy my life.

Kim, Claudette, Mary and Anthony were all informed about the dates. I had phone contact with Mary but didn't tell her where I lived. I never really warmed to her and only kept in touch with her so I could see Hallie. Now that Hallie had left her, I didn't really want to speak to her, but as she made a statement to the police and would be called I didn't dare upset her.

One night I phoned my Auntie Hilary. She knew what was going on and said she wasn't very happy about it. She didn't ask how I was but asked where I was living and if the children were OK.

I said to her, 'Can I ask if you believe me or not?'

Her reply was: 'Don't ask.'

'I just wanted to let you know that during my childhood the best times were spent with you and Granddad,' I said.

I told her I was going to have to go and she said she'd like me to keep in contact. I was a little upset as I felt she just assumed that I was lying. I suppose it's like Karen said: it was not about believing me; it was just more comfortable not to. That means that I will always be the victim. I will have to pay, and even more now, for what they did to me. Will I ever stop paying?

I had spent quite a few evenings crying over Karen, and when I thought about her on my daily drive into London, as I often did, my eyes would fill with tears. We had moved away and I hadn't told her. But I didn't feel so warm towards her now, plus she wasn't talking to me. Perhaps I should have rung her and told her, but then memories of that look she gave me came back. I couldn't tell her, because moving away seemed so final. But now she couldn't contact me even if she wanted to.

I missed my sister so much. We used to phone each other every night and saw each other every weekend, so our falling out had left a big empty gap. I sometimes wondered what I would do if she ever got in touch. Would I be joyful and happy that I had her back? Or would I remember the hurt and say, No thanks, goodbye? Had I been unfair to her? Did I ask her to choose between my father and me? But it wasn't me versus him: it was me versus him and the entire family. I thought about Jake too. Ela was still looking after him while Karen worked. Maybe Karen had done what she had to do.

Working in London was doing me no good at all. I needed

to get a transfer, and quickly. I had to get away from the area, with all the memories. The big question that constantly entered my head was, Am I doing the right thing? But even if I'd decided that I wasn't, it was too late to turn back. Deep down I knew I had to do it. They had robbed me of my childhood, and that's a time that is very precious for everyone. Yet I don't have any happy memories of those years. All I remember is always being scared, too afraid to do anything in case it was wrong. It was a wasted childhood.

The court cases were due to start in just a few weeks' time and my PC came to see me at work. I'd already had a visit from two other police officers earlier that day. On my first day of counselling I'd had to fill up the car. At the same time that I was filling up, the car next to mine had an abducted man in the boot. The policemen wanted to know if I could remember seeing anything.

'No, sorry,' I answered. 'It was six months ago.'

The receptionist gave me a funny look when my PC turned up. I bet she thought I was a right dodgy character.

I told my PC that I was scared in case my brothers turned up at court. Also, I wanted to know if there was a possibility that my dad and stepmother would be able to change their pleas to guilty, so that I wouldn't need to attend court. She told me that it was hardly likely that my brothers would appear and, even if they did, they were not likely to do anything untoward to me. As for my father and stepmother, they would be asked what their pleas were on the first day of court and so, yes, they could plead guilty, but that doesn't happen very often. She told me to stop worrying.

171

She arranged for me to visit the court the following week, just so that I knew what it would look like. Kim and I went. It wasn't as bad as I had pictured it. I had a mental image of a large, grey, stone-walled room with big wooden benches, and the judge would be sitting high up, glaring down at me. It wasn't like that at all. It was a fairly small room and it was carpeted, which made it seem a bit cosier than I'd imagined. The PC showed me where everyone would be. She said that I had to face the jury, which most people find hard to do, as the barristers would be asking me all the questions and they would be situated on my right. I was glad to see the court: it took a few worries from my mind.

On Friday, 13 July I rang the PC in the afternoon to find out whether my dad's case was starting on the Monday. 'No, afraid not,' was her reply.

I was asked to ring back on Monday to see if the case was starting on the Tuesday instead. I was glad it wouldn't be Monday as it was my birthday on the Sunday and for the children's sake I had to try to enjoy it. I was trying to act normally around them but it wasn't easy as most of the time I was shaking and very close to tears.

My boss, Kathy, was aware of what was happening, although she didn't know all the details. She once asked me why I'd only recently stopped going round to my dad's and why I ever took my children round there. My mum had also asked the same question and so had my niece Hallie. I didn't answer them. I knew that all my life I had been blaming my stepmother for everything and had only recently seen my dad as an abuser. It had been easy to blame her, because she wasn't around any more and also because everyone feared her. Nobody hated my dad, though. He was seen as a great father.

As I drove into work on Monday morning I kept thinking, It could be tomorrow. In one way I wanted it to be tomorrow so that it would all be over with sooner, but on the other hand I was dreading having to stand up in court and tell everyone what I used to have to do. I so wanted my dad to plead guilty so that I wouldn't have to testify in court.

By Thursday I was totally pissed off. Not just me, but my bosses, my husband's bosses and Claudette, Kim and Anthony were all on standby in case they were needed in court the next day. I felt that it was a stupid system and just too stressful for everyone. I rang up the PC and asked if we could come off the warned list and get a definite date. She rang me back a little later and told me that she'd had the case removed from the warned list and she would let me know when the first case was due to start. Well, that was a big relief. The 'warned' system had only piled extra pressure on me and I was already in an extremely nervous state. We could all relax a little now as we knew that we would be given a couple of weeks' notice.

One night I spoke to Anthony and told him about my phone call with Auntie Hilary and how she never asked about how I was or what had happened. He told me that older people don't like to talk about sex with their children or grandchildren. I suppose he was right and I never said any more, but inside I was hurt. Anthony also told me that Dad had been told that if he pleaded guilty he could get 12 months but if he were found guilty he could get up to two years. Also, the PC had told Kim that, should he be found guilty, she doubted that he'd get a long sentence as it had all happened so long ago.

On Thursday, 16 August I was told that the first court case would be starting on Monday, 1 October. My dad's case would probably be two days and my stepmother's three days, I told Kathy.

'That's not too far away,' she said, before adding, with her very next breath, 'Sue, I'm sorry, but I have to give someone else your job and put you back on to the Ops floor. I really don't have any choice in the matter.'

I couldn't believe it. 'Is there absolutely nothing that can be done?' I asked.

Apparently there wasn't. My position as LA was on a six-month contract, which was renewed at the end of each term. But I had been there nearly two years and the system was that at the end of that time the job would be officially mine. However, another office nearby had closed and there was an LA who needed to be relocated. And because Royal Mail has a rule that, if an office closes down, the company will relocate the staff to the nearest available office, she was to have my job. I was gutted. I was two weeks away from the job officially being mine. My thoughts went back to when I was first offered the position. I didn't particularly want it and I even took a pay cut. What a kick in the teeth! I went up to see the top man.

I was very close to tears but asked him if there was anything that could be done.

There wasn't. I went back downstairs. Kathy was there with our head of department, and I told them how I felt. I also told them, 'Royal Mail will lose out in the end as you will not find anyone as good as me to do my job.' I felt that this was so true. I'd always had everything under control. I'd given them 110 per cent. Andy, the head of department, said, 'Don't take it personally.'

What a stupid thing to say! Of course I'm going to take it personally – I do with everything else in life.

Kathy tried to comfort me. 'You still have a job,' she said. 'It's not like you're out of work.'

I was hurt. I loved working for Royal Mail and was really grateful for all the help they had given me. I felt that Kathy must have known for a while but didn't say anything until the court dates had been decided, which was good of her. But it still felt like a massive slap in the face. I had two more days to go and then I was due to take two weeks' holiday. My replacement was due to start on the Monday. Kathy asked me if, when I returned, I would train the new lady.

'It'll give you a couple more weeks off the floor,' she said, as if doing me a great favour, when really I knew that she couldn't be expected to be familiar with all the details of what I'd done.

On the Friday before my holiday I rang a few of my favourite customers and Royal Mail co-workers and said goodbye. Then I received a call from a customer with a query about delays in delivery. He had been sending in his mail without the dockets and so his mail was always 'on hold' until the next day. I explained the process to him.

'I'd better get someone in for the evenings to do my paperwork, then,' he said.

'Just out of interest, how much are you offering?'

'Why? Are you interested?'

'Oh, yes,' I replied and explained my recent setback with Royal Mail.

'Come and have a chat with me,' he said.

'Well, I'm on holiday next week, so how about Monday?' I asked.

'No, I'm in Oxford on Monday,' he explained.

'Oh, I live near there. I moved there a couple of months ago.'

'OK. Monday at eleven o'clock.'

'See you then,' I said.

I told my workmates Vincent and Vivien, and they helped me scrape together a CV. I then went round and said goodbye to a few people. 'Just in case I don't return,' I said.

They all knew how unhappy I was about the way things had turned out. I wasn't optimistic about my new job opportunity and at the same time I felt that I couldn't come back and train someone else to do my job – and to go back on the floor to do it! Even though I had asked to go back on the floor in my request for a transfer to my local office, I just couldn't do it there. I couldn't travel all that way just to pick up a sack from one place and put it in another place. No. I would spend the next two weeks looking for something else. I really didn't want the hassle of job hunting and going for interviews as I was still immensely stressed about the court cases. I couldn't see any employer taking on a 'nervous wreck'! I didn't need all this right now.

I woke up on Monday morning with my normal feeling of self-hate. I wasn't going to go for my interview. 'What on earth would he want me for?' I asked myself. But I went – I had to. Just imagine how weak it would have sounded when Darren asked me how I got on. 'Well, I didn't have the bottle to go.' No, I'd give it a try.

I had a chat with a chap called Mike. Even though his company was based in Slough, he had a contract with a leading high-street retailer in Oxfordshire and he needed someone to be in charge of posting all their internet orders.

'I can do that,' I told him.

He offered me the job. I'd be working in Cowley, 35 miles nearer home than the Royal Mail job, and the wage was a massive 25 per cent more. *Yes!* I would be in charge of dispatching all their parcels through Royal Mail, Business Express or Securicor. I also had to do the dockets and keep records. I couldn't believe my luck. A huge weight had lifted from my shoulders. No more travelling into London every day and getting depressed on the way.

Mike asked when I could start.

'I'm on holiday for two weeks and then I have to give a month's notice,' I said. I had to work out quickly how many weeks that would be and if that took me up to my court dates. 'Does 8 October sound OK?' I asked. I couldn't tell my new employer that I was needed in court the week before that. It just wouldn't look good.

'That's fine,' he said and shook my hand.

I was so happy. I was about to drive home when Kathy rang. She needed to know about certain procedures. Even though she was my manager, she didn't have a clue. But then she never needed to as I always made sure that everything ran smoothly. She told me that she couldn't wait for me to get back and get this new woman trained.

I could now enjoy my fortnight off. I took the kids to Norfolk to see Claudette. She had two little girls and they called me Auntie Sue. They were my family now. Claudette told me that Steven, my younger brother, had become a father. Her father had been to see his newborn granddaughter in hospital, where he bumped into Steven, who was visiting his wife Nita and their newborn baby. I was upset. I hated hearing things about the family as there wasn't anything that I could do about it.

When my two weeks were over I phoned in sick. I just couldn't go back. My stomach was already in knots at the thought of it. Not just to work, but back to Greenford. I went to see my doctor, who told me that I looked a lot better and asked me why. I didn't have to do all that travelling any more, I told him. I also said it wasn't just the travelling that was a problem but the fact that I was based in Greenford, less than five minutes from my dad's house. There was always the possibility that I could bump into him or anyone else in the family. He wrote me a sick note covering me for the whole month. He knew the court cases were coming up and wanted to keep me as calm as possible. I sent my resignation letter and my sick note to Kathy. She phoned me to ask if I was OK and we said goodbye.

Now that I was in between jobs I suddenly found a huge amount of time on my hands. Time to think and worry about things. At least work had taken my mind off things a little.

Darren and I drove up to meet the kids from school. A car overtook us and went roaring up the road. Darren said to me, 'He's a right wanker. Every day he does that.' It must have really riled him, because he hardly ever swears. While we were waiting for our children I saw Mr Wanker. He was a big skinhead with tattoos all up his arms. His son, aged six or seven, tripped over something and would definitely have fallen flat on his face if his father's protective arm hadn't instinctively come out to stop him. I watched them both go back to their car, the little boy holding on tightly to his daddy's hand. To me, Mr Wanker wasn't such a bad guy.

The first court case was looming. All my anxieties had now doubled in size. I didn't want to stand up in court and tell everyone what he'd done to me. I was in Tesco's and suddenly found that I couldn't breathe. I had to go back to the fruit and veg section and tear off a mushroom bag to breathe into. Later I went to the doctor's again. He asked me if I smoked. 'No, I gave up nine months ago,' I answered proudly, expecting him to be full of praise for my achievement.

'Well done, but why on earth did you choose to pack up in what is going to be the most stressful year of your life?'

I didn't know what to say and so I just said, 'Sorry!'

He gave me some tablets for anxiety.

By now I was at the stage where I wasn't regretting pressing charges. I just wanted it all to be over. Oddly enough, I wasn't at all bothered about my stepmother's case. It was my dad's that petrified me. I really don't know why. I kept telling myself that it was only for one day, maybe even only a few hours.

The weeks had slipped by and it was now the weekend before the case was due to start. Claudette, her husband Steve and their two little girls arrived at my home on the Sunday. Kim had already arrived earlier. They were all going to stay with me and look after my two while I was in court, and then

I'd look after Claudette's girls while she was in court. I couldn't believe that the time had now come. This time tomorrow it could all be over, I said to myself.

Claudette, Kim and I were chatting when Katy, Claudette's four-year-old daughter, came into the room. She looked so small and innocent. I had been like that once. I must keep reminding myself of that, I thought, and just forget the fact that he's my father.

Around 1am we all went to bed. I'd had only one glass of wine as I didn't want to turn up at court hungover and bleary-eyed. The PC had told us all that I would be called in on the first day and Claudette, Kim and Mary on the second day. Claudette and Kim were to be my babysitters for the day as Darren would be with me. He and I slept downstairs but I couldn't sleep. I could barely breathe. It felt like someone was standing on my chest. I tried to fill up my lungs with air but couldn't quite fill them all the way up. It reminded me of a 'Hit the Bell' stall at a fairground. You could hit the hammer so hard and the little red disc would go zooming up to the top, but more often than not it would stop short of the target.

I was so scared. I could be sending my dad to prison. What sort of person would do that to her own father? A dad who took me in when my own mother couldn't keep me. But he was a dad who totally misused his position. The fact that he was my dad just made it seem all the worse. He'd also known about my stepmother's physical abuse and had chosen to do nothing. If he had been a stranger in court tomorrow, it would have been a lot easier. It would still have been hard, but manageable. I was also very afraid that my brothers would be there.

SEVENTEEN

All night I tossed and turned. As soon as I thought of another 'what if?' question, numerous answers would appear at the other side of my head. I was having a right old battle in there! I never slept at all. At 4am I thought to myself, At least in 12 hours' time it will all be over.

Steve had to get up at six and travel to work. Darren and I also got up then. I got dressed and put my emergency hanky in my pocket. My hands were already starting to tremble. I wanted to take one of my stress balls but I decided that I might look a bit odd with my pocket bulging out with such a large round lump. I went in to see Kim and then Claudette. They both wished me luck. I was close to tears. I so didn't want to do it. I still hoped that my dad would change his plea so that I wouldn't have to go through with it.

We got to the court around 9am. We had to walk through a metal detector. Then we had to go to the victim support room, from where we would be called into court. As the room was solely for witnesses there was no chance of my dad being there. I told the lady at the desk who I was and she asked if I'd rung on Friday to make sure that the case was starting today.

'No. I didn't know that I had to,' I answered.

My policewoman turned up just as I was being told to go home and come back again tomorrow. I couldn't believe it. I had to go through all that again. Then the PC explained that my dad's case would be starting at two that afternoon but I wouldn't be needed as they had to swear in the jury and go over procedures.

Back home we went. I'd had my heart set on it all being over with that day. But at least I knew that I would be called in first thing the next morning and, hopefully, finished by the afternoon. Deep inside me I still hoped that he would plead guilty. We got back home and I just went to bed and slept. That night I was thinking about my dad and how he was coping. I bet he's hoping that I won't turn up tomorrow, I thought.

We arrived at the court about the same time as before. I was told that they would start at ten o'clock and I would probably be called at eleven. A victim support worker attached herself to me; wherever I went she went. I was so nervous I had to go to the loo what seemed like every five minutes. After a while she would just wait outside. Darren was going to come into court with me, but the victim support lady and the PC both advised against it. They didn't want Darren glaring angrily at my father, which naturally he would do once he'd heard everything. So it was decided that he would stay in the victim support room until I returned.

'When I'm called I have to just get up and go. Don't hug me or even look at me or I'll just burst,' I told him.

He nodded. He knew how close to the edge I was.

While we were waiting I had to read over my statement. Seeing it again in black and white made it become even more real. It was horrible what he'd done. I looked round and noticed pictures drawn by kiddies. They must have gone through this procedure too, poor little things.

The PC appeared at the door. Oh God, this is it, I thought to myself. Behind her came another lady wearing a black gown and wig.

'Sue, this is our barrister,' the PC said. 'She just wanted to meet you before we started.'

'Are we nearly ready then?' I asked.

'Yes. They're just having a short break and then you'll be called. I just wanted to say hello, and just remember, all you're doing is telling the truth,' the barrister said.

'OK,' I answered. I couldn't help looking down to the ground. My dad hadn't pleaded guilty, then. I didn't really think he would; it was more of a tiny desperate little hope that he might.

The court usher appeared at the door (which I had been staring at constantly all morning) and called my name. I stood up and followed the lady. I didn't look at Darren but just stared ahead. As I walked down the corridor I really did think that my ankles were going to snap. Every step I took I was gingerly putting my foot down, I felt so weak and empty. Whatever I do, I mustn't cry, I told myself.

We walked into the courtroom. I felt everyone's eyes suddenly on me and, in my overwhelming shyness, I just looked down at the ground. Ela was there, but no brothers, which was a big relief. I got to the witness box. My dad was to the right of me. He was at the very back of the room, behind a security shield, and had a security man sitting next to him. I had to stand and face the jury. The judge was to my left, the defence and prosecuting barristers were to my right, my dad behind them and Ela on a bench just behind me. I was given the Bible and shown a card which I had to read out. It was the Oath. I got it wrong, I was so nervous. I wanted all the words to come out quickly. The quicker everything was done, the quicker I could get out of there. The judge said I was allowed to sit. I was grateful for that as my legs were trembling so much that I felt they would give way any minute. We started.

The family tree, the one that was drawn when I first met the PC, had been photocopied and everyone in the courtroom had one. I was given mine and asked if the details were correct.

'Yes, sir,' I answered. I didn't know what to call him.

The barrister asked me to tell the court about my childhood. So I did. I couldn't look at the jury, though. It was just too awkward, because the barrister kept asking me questions and when you answer someone you look at him or her. I told them everything. If I forgot anything the barrister would ask me a related question, to make me remember. The judge asked if I wanted a break.

'No, thanks,' I answered. I just wanted to say what I had to say and get out of there. My barrister stood up and said that we were nearly finished anyway.

All I said really was what was on my statement. I did squirm a bit when I had to describe certain incidents. And as I didn't know the correct terminology for some incidents, I stumbled a bit. On the whole, I think I managed to get everything out. I had to explain what I actually had to do on some occasions and I didn't know how to say it. In my language I would say that I had to jerk him off, but I couldn't say that in a court of law. So I said I masturbated him. Was that right? Didn't masturbate mean playing with yourself? I didn't know. I wished I'd spent some time thinking about what I was going to say but I had always clung on to the hope that I would never be needed in court. Luckily, they never said anything about it. The judge said we could break for lunch. I left my box but was gently pushed back in by the usher. I wasn't supposed to leave until the judge had left the room. How was I supposed to know that?

I was a bit surprised at how easy it had been. Once I started it all seemed to flow out. I'd had my mind focused on a little girl. I actually pictured Claudette's little Katy. We went and sat in the car. I phoned home and spoke to Claudette and Kim. I couldn't go into details, as I wasn't allowed to talk about the case with other witnesses. I just told them that I was fine and ready for the next round. But I knew that my dad's barrister was going to tear into me.

We had to return to our little room and again wait to be called. I wasn't so nervous now. I was just so anxious to get it all over and done with in the one day. The usher appeared. Here we go again.

The defence barrister started by asking me about my stepmother's treatment of me. I told him that she was a scary lady. He nodded sympathetically. What's he up to? I thought to myself. And then I knew.

'And so you're angry with your father for not stopping his wife from mistreating you?'

'No,' I answered. 'He was hardly ever there and, besides, she was never nasty to me in front of others.'

He then started going on about how I felt when Ela took my children out. She had recently started to do this because sometimes there would be a meeting at work that I just couldn't get out of. I told him that I liked Ela having the children but was not very happy about her taking them out as then I would worry about them.

'And so you would rather your own children were in the home, with your father, even though you're accusing him of gross indecencies?'

I had to explain that at the time I felt that everything that had happened to me as a child was entirely my fault and it was only recently, actually during counselling, that I had realised that it wasn't.

The barrister told me that I was making everything up.

'No,' I answered. 'Why would I lie?'

'I'll get back to that in a minute,' he replied. He then starting asking questions about my natural mother and how my relationship with her was progressing. I told him that it wasn't really.

'Is that because she lives so far away?'

'No. It's because I'll never forgive her for leaving me there.'

The barrister was at a loss as to where to go next. I now knew that my father must have told everyone that my real mum was behind everything. He then tried to get back on to my stepmother's abuse and how angry I must have been.

'Yes, but his abuse was worse because he's my real dad,' I said sadly.

The barrister asked for a short break. This time I waited for the judge to leave the room and then I left. I didn't really want a break as I was on a high. Everything the barrister had tried to throw at me I'd just hit right back at him. It hadn't been nearly as bad as I'd imagined. I remembered the PC's and the prosecution barrister's words: 'Remember, all you're doing is telling the truth.' I was very anxious to get back in there. Time was moving on. I knew that judges liked to finish at four. It was nearly three now. After 15 minutes we were called back in.

The barrister asked, 'How was it, in a house where five other people lived, that no one else knew about what you claimed to be happening?'

'My dad had the room downstairs and all our rooms had locks on the doors.'

He quickly changed the subject.

When he asked if I'd ever left my children at my dad's home when they were babies, I told him, 'No. It's not that I never left them there. I never left them anywhere, not even with my husband.'

I don't really know what he was leading up to, but whatever it was he gave up. I looked at my dad, who was sitting with his hands over his face. For the first time ever I felt that this big, disgusting secret of mine was now his problem. He now had to deal with it. For me it was over. I had given it back to the rightful owner. I felt relieved but I also felt sorry for him. He was now going to have to go through a little of what I'd been through.

That was the last time I saw my father. The judge said we could go.

The victim support lady said I'd done well and told me, 'Yes, you got him.'

The PC came up and told me that I'd done brilliantly. I wasn't joyous. I was so glad that it was all over but sorry that it had come to this. I also thought that my dad might have just done one good thing for me and pleaded guilty so as not to put me through that. But it really hadn't been that bad. After all the nervousness had gone I just did what I had to do: I answered their questions. I had to tell them all my deep secrets but I'd already told Susan, my counsellor, and so it wasn't as if I was telling it all for the first time. At times tears had crept into the corners of my eyes but I'd made sure that I held them back. I didn't want my dad to say I'd swayed the jury with my tears. He was guilty and I needed to prove it. People had previously said to me, 'You'll have your day in court.' I'd thought that was a load of bollocks. I didn't want a day in court. I now knew what they meant.

We drove home. I wanted to see my children as soon as possible. I phoned Claudette and Kim. They both told me that they had received a call from the PC telling them that they would not be needed for this case. I was glad. And I was very grateful to them for agreeing to do it, but it was a very nerve-racking experience.

I felt like I should be joyous and celebrating the fact that it was all over, but I just wasn't in the mood. The PC rang me and told me that they would be calling Anthony.

'Why?' I asked, remembering that he had told me that he would never say anything against his dad.

'I can't say, but it's nothing to worry about,' she replied.

I was worried about Anthony. I poured myself out a large glass of wine and told Claudette and Kim everything that had happened. Now they were not needed as witnesses, I could tell them everything. Mary rang me and told me that she also had been told that she would not be needed in court.

That night Anthony rang me and said that he had just received a message telling him that he was needed in court the next day.

'Is it Mum's case already?' he asked.

'No. It's still Dad's.'

'Why are they calling me then?'

'I don't really know. I asked her but she wasn't allowed to tell me,' I said. And then I blurted out, 'When I originally made my statement I told her that I'd been and seen you, and you said that you'd all had your suspicions about what was going on. I don't know but maybe that's why they're calling you. I'm really sorry. Are you going to be all right?'

'I'll just have to be, won't I?' he answered. He didn't sound very happy.

I felt really bad, but there wasn't anything I could do about it.

I still had a few days off, my best friends were with me, the kids were fine, and Darren, even though he never said much about it, was, I knew, glad that it was over. I did have a little drink that night. I was so glad that it was over and, even though there was a possibility that I could be sending my father to prison, I did have a great feeling of achievement. I had done it.

The PC promised to ring me at the end of each day to keep me informed of what was going on. She called and told me that

Anthony hadn't turned up but she'd had a chat with him and he would be coming tomorrow. She told me also that my brother Paul had stood up in court and said that he knew that his dad couldn't do such a thing. And the wife of one of my dad's old drinking mates had stood up and said that she used to send her two girls round to my dad's. Neither of them did much good for my dad's case as I'd never claimed that they knew. I was a bit upset over Paul's evidence, for he suspected what went on, but then I knew Paul. He would have done anything to get his dad's love. I did feel that it was unfair that I wasn't allowed to know whom the defence was calling in and yet they had to know all our witnesses.

It didn't really matter. I had said in my statement that over the years I'd told Claudette, Kim and Mary but no one else, which was the truth.

Thursday morning approached. Not only was I now anxious about the current court case but I was also supposed to be starting my new job on the following Monday and we still had another court case to do.

The PC rang me at dinnertime and told me that it had been my dad's turn to defend himself. I told her that I didn't want to know what he'd said about me as I knew that I'd only be hurt and angry. She did tell me that he had answered in a cocky, arrogant manner, which didn't do him any favours. I asked how Anthony had been.

'He was in the dock for barely a minute,' she replied. 'The prosecution wanted to back up your claim that your father wasn't around much when you were younger, that's all. OK? The jury is out now and so I'll speak to you as soon as I hear anything.'

I didn't really expect her to call me that day.

Claudette and her family left at dinnertime. I gave them all a hug and said thanks.

'What for?' asked Claudette. 'You did it all by yourself.'

'For being here,' I answered. As much as I love my husband and children, they didn't know me when I was younger and what I was like growing up. Claudette and Kim had been my friends for years, so they knew me and they remembered things. They often said that, looking back, it just seemed so obvious that something was very wrong. Again this made it all seem real. 'I'll call you as soon as I hear anything,' I told Claudette.

We did hear, that very afternoon. The PC rang me and told me that my dad been found guilty on six out of the eight charges. He was now on his way to prison and would be on remand for one month before being sentenced.

I asked her what he was found 'not guilty' on. She told me that the jury might have found it hard to believe that I could remember incidents that occurred when I was just four years old. She told me that my stepmother's case had now been cancelled for six weeks and would take place sometime in November. As soon as she had a definite date she would let me know.

'Thanks,' I said and hung up.

Darren and Kim were anxiously waiting for me to tell them.

'Guilty on six out of the eight,' I told them. Kim broke down and Darren came and hugged me. I was just numb. I had to let it slowly sink in. All I wanted to hear was the word 'guilty'. That was all that mattered to me. Yes, he was guilty and it really, officially, wasn't my fault. I had been believed. All those years that I'd kept it bottled up inside me – what a waste of my life! My dad now being locked up wasn't going to give me back those wasted years. It wasn't a joyful victory. I didn't feel the urge to dance around the room or anything. My dad was on his way to prison. I had completely forgotten about the way I'd felt about him over the past 18 months and was now very worried about him. I never wanted him to go to prison but really to face up to his problem and get help. He would never, ever do that. Who would admit to being a child abuser? But at least now he was well away from other innocent little girls.

I rang round my Geordie family and all my other friends who knew what was going on. They all practically said the same thing: 'That's where he belongs.' If I'd read the story in a newspaper I would have said the same thing, but it's very different when it's your own family. I was very numb. It was a bittersweet feeling. I was very glad that I had finally got my justice and my abuser was being punished for his crimes, but it was my dad and it would affect my family.

Kim went back home the next day. I thanked her and said things were going to be all right now. We had to get our lives back to normal. I would be starting my new job on Monday and so we had to get back into a routine. We told the children that Granddad was now in prison. They had always known that my stepmother wasn't a very nice person but had only recently found out that their granddad too was not a very nice man. They didn't know exactly what he had done, for we felt that they were much too young to understand, but they knew that it was serious. I'm immensely proud of my children. Over the past few years they had seen me sad and tearful a lot, and both of them would keep coming up to me and kissing and hugging me and they did make me feel better. I'd lost the Hamford family but I had my children and my husband.

Someone mentioned to me that he would be searched for drugs before he entered prison.

'Yeah, I know,' I said.

'Yes, but do you know exactly where they search?'

And then the penny dropped. I was upset that my dad could be going through that humiliating process.

'But what about the humiliating things he made you do?'

Yes, that was true, but it didn't make it any easier. I didn't like it and I wouldn't wish it on anyone else.

EIGHTEEN

When I started my new job on the Monday, I was dying to get back into a routine. My hours were 11am to 7pm, Monday to Friday. It was OK and it certainly took my mind off things. I worked at first with another colleague but he eventually disappeared. I was left to run things by myself, which I much preferred. My job was to make sure all the parcels left on time, records were updated and the customer was kept happy. I liked it. I didn't have a manager hovering over my shoulder all the time. I didn't have any more boring meetings to attend. I went, did what I had to do and then left. It was so nice not having to travel into London and back every day.

I rang Anthony one night to see how he was. I told him that I was fine and that I wished I could go to the press, just to let other people know that things can be sorted out.

He said, 'You've got what you wanted. Just let it go. Think about Karen, Steven, Ela and even me and how it would affect us if it all got out. The Hamford name is not very common. A man here at work told me that his brother's house was set alight just because he had the same name as a paedophile that had been "Named and Shamed" in the *News of the World*.'

'OK,' I said. I wanted to ask how everyone was but didn't feel that this was the right time. I asked if he was OK after the case and he said that he was very frightened in court but just stood up, was asked one question, answered it and left. I asked him how he felt about meeting his mother again.

'I just want it over with,' he said.

'I imagine her to be a little old lady now. Just like her mother. Remember her? I asked.

We chatted for a little while and said goodbye. I didn't know it but that was the last conversation I was to have with my brother.

Four weeks later the PC rang me.

'How did it go?' I asked.

'Very well. He got 12 months for every guilty charge, but they have to run consecutively. So that meant six years in total. The judge has recommended that he serve two-thirds of this sentence and he has to sign the Sex Offenders Register.'

'Was any of the family there?'

'No. Nobody was there. With regard to your stepmother's case it has now been postponed until January as her defence have asked for your medical reports.'

'But surely they should have got everything by now. What if the case had started when it was meant to, back in July?'

'I know,' she said. 'The judge told them exactly the same thing. I'll let you know the exact date.'

Immediately after the PC's call I rang Darren. I was shaking. Six years is a long time. Surely now the family could see how serious this was, I said. Darren was, like I'd been, a bit surprised at the length of the sentence.

'But look at how long you've had to deal with it,' he said.

That was true. I rang everyone and told them. Kim said that when she'd given her statement the PC had told her that, as there wasn't any sign of him abusing anyone else since, he would probably receive the minimum sentence.

My friend Wendy's abuser had been found guilty on several charges involving a number of girls and he was given 12 months for each charge, but his sentences were to run concurrently and so with good behaviour he'd be out in six to nine months. Everyone was rather shocked at my dad's sentence. I thought about my stepmother and how she must be feeling. We hadn't any eyewitnesses for my dad's case and yet he was now in prison. We had witnesses for her case, so I was sure she was really freaking out now.

The following week a lady from the probation service called round to see me. She told me that, owing to the judge's recommendation, my dad would probably have to serve four years, unless he was really ill or there were any other exceptional circumstances. I would be informed of his release six months prior to that. I asked her if he could appeal and if I would be needed in court again.

'Yes, he can appeal, but I really don't see any justification for it. The trial was fair and he got a fair sentence. If he did then, no, you wouldn't be needed in court again. It would go before a panel of judges who would go over everything and then

197

decide.' She went on, 'He's in prison now point-blankly refusing to admit his crimes. There is a rehabilitation programme that he can go on, but he refuses. He's doing himself no favours, because if he wants an early release then he's got to show willingness to help himself.'

'What happens when he does come out?' I asked. 'I mean, what does being on the Sex Offenders Register actually entail?'

'When he comes out he may not be allowed to go home straight away. He may have to stay in a halfway house until we're satisfied that he will not reoffend. But until the six years is completed he will not have any unsupervised contact with children. If he does break the rules, then he will have to return to prison. Being on the register will allow social services and the police to know who and where he is.'

She said goodbye for now and that she would call me in a few years' time.

I looked at Darren. We didn't say very much. It just seemed so heavy.

I spent the next few weeks worrying about my dad. He would have to face Christmas in prison. How horrible! But I was now comforting myself with the fact that his actions put him where he was and not my words.

Several weeks later it was the kids' half-term holiday. I rang up Elaine on a Friday night to arrange for her kids to stay. Karen no longer worked for Elaine but she was still very much in contact with her.

'Hello, Sue. How did it go?

'How did what go?' I asked.

'Oh, I thought you were ringing up about the appeal hearing.'

'No. I didn't know there was one,' I told her.

All weekend I was worried about it. It wasn't so much about my dad being released from prison but more: 'Oh, we got it wrong'. I wouldn't have been able to cope with an appeal hearing that went in his favour.

The appeal was heard. The original guilty verdict stood.

Mary rang me one day while I was at work.

'Guess who I've just bumped into?' she asked.

'Don't know. Who?'

'The Johnsons.'

'Did you speak to them?'

'Yes. I told them all about Allan. They were really shocked, so much so that he had to sit down. She said she wished that she had known, as she would have done something about it. I told them that you were up in court next over your stepmother.'

'Is that for the beatings?' he had asked Mary.

'Yes,' she had said.

'That didn't come as a big shock to them,' Mary told me.

I thought about them and sent them a Christmas card, just to say Hi. I told them that they weren't to know, as nobody knew, and that I was OK now and looking forward to enjoying the rest of my life.

I had been to my GP quite a few times over the past few months. My blood pressure was a little high, not alarmingly so, but it needed checking. With the court cases, moving house and losing my Royal Mail job, stress was blamed. However, my drinking had again crept up to an every-night occurrence and

I'd get drunk two, maybe three, times a week. My doctor sent me to an addictions counsellor to try to help me gain a little control over my drinking. I'd been sort of hoping that once the court cases were over I wouldn't need to drink any more.

The second court case had again been cancelled and I just felt like it would never be over. I went to meet my new counsellor. I was hoping to meet someone similar to Susan, but it wasn't quite the same circumstances. I didn't have to go into details this time but just give a brief outline. I told the counsellor why I drank and about the court cases and she asked if she could refer me to her colleague, who could do much more for me.

'OK,' I said. When the letter arrived offering me an appointment I wasn't going to go. She had so many letters after her name that I felt that as soon as I walked into the room she would be able to easily read me and instantly know everything. I met her and she was OK. She was also called Susan. I told her that, as much as I tried to reason with myself, I still felt very mean. Why could I not forgive him? Why did I have to report him to the police? I had read the Dave Pelzer series and he had forgiven his parents; he had even named his own son after his father. Why couldn't I forgive? And why was my dad still refusing to admit that he'd done anything wrong?

'But, Sue, he never asked to be forgiven. You've said yourself that he saw it as his right. Look at when he was caught shoplifting: he saw it as his right. A man that can excuse himself for stealing is not going to admit to ever doing anything wrong.'

She was right. He would never, ever admit to it, I knew deep down.

The second court case had been due to start on 28 January but had again been postponed for a week.

Kim arrived on the Sunday before. I was so glad to have her with me as she knew my stepmother. I could talk to her about it and she knew.

Darren and I drove to the court on Monday morning. I just wasn't that bothered about my stepmother's case. I was exhausted. For the past three years it had been constantly on my mind. I just wanted it over with once and for all. We got there at about nine and were told that we wouldn't be needed for two hours, so we went for a coffee. Outside my stepmother's courtroom I noticed a dark-haired man sitting there.

'How old do you reckon he is?' I asked Darren.

'Maybe 40,' he replied. 'Why?'

'It must be Andy Evans,' I said. 'Her husband.'

Again we had to wait in the witness room. I was given my statement and told to read it thoroughly. I tried. Again they were very strong memories. I didn't need my statement to remind me of what she had done. My PC called me out. We needed to have a chat with our barrister. Our last one couldn't do this case and so we had a new guy. He took us into a little room and told me that I wasn't, under any circumstances, allowed to mention my dad's case. I was also not allowed to mention the 'torn-off ear' or the 'broken arm'. Although in her statement she did admit to accidentally breaking it, because I couldn't actually remember the incidents and I didn't have any medical records, they couldn't prove who caused the injuries or even if they were done at all, even though I had the scars to prove it happened.

'OK,' I said.

Fifteen minutes later I was called in.

It had gone eleven and so I knew that I wouldn't be in there for that long. I walked in and took the Oath. I glanced at her. She wasn't looking in my direction but it was her. She hadn't changed at all. My stomach started to tremble and my legs started to shake. The judge told me that he would like me to remain standing so that the jury could hear me better. Standing did not help at all.

One of the first things my barrister asked was: 'How did you remember the exact broadcasting time of a cartoon over 20 years later?'

'It was because it was such a big thing for me to be allowed to stay up and watch it,' I answered. I then had to tell the court everything that had happened. I didn't want to look at her, and was trying to pretend that she wasn't there, but occasionally I caught sight of her. As she was sitting right behind the barrister it was hard, impossible, not to catch the occasional glimpse. Her barrister was scribbling away and kept asking the judge to tell me to speak up.

We broke for lunch. I saw her walking down the corridor. I so wanted to go up to her and say, 'I'm not a scared little girl any more.' But I couldn't, probably because I was still petrified of her. Even though I was five foot ten and massively built – I prefer that description to just being called 'fat' – and could have flattened her with one punch, I was still very much that scared little girl.

After lunch it was her barrister's turn to launch into me, and she did, big time.

The first thing she said was: 'You also claimed that your

father sexually abused you. But that's not true, is it, Mrs Owen?'

I couldn't answer. I was told not to. I looked at my PC. She was glaring at the barrister. I looked up at the judge. I didn't know what to say or do.

'Yes, he did,' I answered.

The judge intervened and told her to stop.

The barrister then said that, if I was always in my room and wasn't allowed meals, how was it that I was claiming that she treated me strictly at the tea table?

In my mind I thought that I would surely be dead if she hadn't fed me during the holidays, but I just couldn't say it out loud. I wanted to get out of there as quickly as possible and get back to my normal life and never have to think about my stepmother ever again.

The barrister said that I'd lied about being kicked when *Paddington Bear* was on. She asked me, 'What shoes did your stepmother wear?'

'Wooden flip-flop ones,' I answered.

'But Mrs Evans never wore shoes, did she?'

I couldn't believe it. I couldn't say anything but just stared at her, wondering if she herself wasn't slightly mad. She also claimed that I'd had short hair throughout my childhood and so she couldn't possibly have spun me round like I'd claimed.

I remembered the photo, the one that I hated, of me with long, wavy hair. She then started asking me about certain teachers in high school.

'Do you remember Mr Green? Mr Harris? Mrs Williams?'

I smiled when she said the last name as I absolutely hated this teacher. She had tried to keep me in for detention once, silly woman, because I'd jumped out of the window and gone round to the front of the building to wave goodbye to her.

'Yes, I remember them,' I answered, wondering what on earth was going to come next.

'Your school reports were all good when you were living with your stepmother.'

I wanted to say, 'Yeah, so I'm not the first person to misbehave in high school.' But I couldn't. I needed to keep control and not offer any unnecessary information. She then got on to my drink problem and said that I had sat around with my new sisters and thought about ways of getting my own back on my stepmother, because deep down I felt hurt that she'd left me.

I just looked at her. I really couldn't believe what I was hearing.

'No,' I replied. How do these people sleep at night? I thought to myself.

She then said, 'Is it not true, Mrs Owen, that, when you knew that your stepmother was pregnant with your sister, you told her that you'd wished the baby was dead?'

'No. I would never say that,' I answered. Christ! I was only seven years old at the time.

Things were going horribly wrong. I was shaking like a leaf the entire time, although I was trying very hard not to as I didn't want the jury to think that I was having alcoholic withdrawal symptoms.

Unfortunately I made a mistake with the sex-abuse charges. I had to go through the incidents again. I hated it and really wished now that I hadn't told the PC. I had to say the word 'vagina' several times. It was deadly embarrassing. Even though during my dad's case I had to say 'penis', it didn't seem as bad as 'vagina'. I had said that the banana that my stepmother used to make me insert in her was peeled, when in fact in my statement I'd said unpeeled (or vice versa). The barrister immediately got hold of that and said that I'd been lying and, as I'd been lying about that, I'd been lying about all the other alleged incidents.

'No!' I said. 'I've made a small mistake, that's all.' I couldn't say that I couldn't remember if the damn thing was peeled or not, because I was scared in case she said that all the other charges could then be considered doubtful.

It was horrible. For the first time I knew how other victims felt when they had said that it had felt like they were the one on trial. I tore out of that courtroom. I wished that I hadn't packed up smoking now as I could really have done with a ciggie.

I had to return. Still, it was three o'clock, so there would only be one more hour to go – for today anyway.

The defence barrister then started on my mental health. 'How did you feel about going to a mental hospital, Mrs Owen?'

'I didn't go to one,' I answered.

'Surely, Mrs Owen, you must have seen the mental health signs at the hospital when you went to see your first psychiatrist?'

'No, I didn't go to a hospital. I went to a clinic in Hanwell and I didn't know that she was a psychiatrist, I thought she was a counsellor,' I answered.

With that my barrister stood up and addressed the judge about the contents of the doctor's reports which had come from the clinic.

'You will see, your honour, that I have been extremely

lenient with my outlining but it is stressed that Mrs Owen does not suffer from hallucinations.'

No, don't be lenient – give them all you got, I was screaming to myself.

We then had to stop for the day. Fuck, fuck, fuck. I so didn't want to come back tomorrow. I saw my PC and told her about the photo.

'Bring it in,' she said.

We drove home. I was not very happy. I was kicking myself all the way home. I felt that I was losing it. All the things I had wanted to say just wouldn't come out. 'Yes' or 'no' answers, that was all I could give. I phoned Kim to tell her that we were on our way. She said that the PC had called her and told her to be at court tomorrow by dinnertime.

It was not a good night at all. I was angry and frustrated. How could another woman defend such an evil person?

We went in the next morning. We were looking for a space to park the car when we noticed Anthony, but he didn't see us. I also spotted my stepmother.

'There she is,' I told Darren. 'Another one of your mother-in-laws.'

We managed to park and walked into court. We walked right past Anthony's car but again he was looking in the other direction. I didn't like to knock on the window and say hello as I now suspected that he wasn't too keen on speaking to me. We went to our little room again. Anthony appeared 20 minutes later and confirmed my suspicions. He didn't acknowledge us at all, even though he had to sit right next to Darren. I was distraught. Maybe he thought that we were not allowed to talk to each other until after the case, I thought, but inside I knew this wasn't the case. I felt so hurt and also very guilty. Anthony had obviously seen the effect that my dad's imprisonment had had on the rest of the family and was perhaps wishing that he had listened to his partner and not got involved. I really wanted to go over and give him a hug, but I couldn't.

I was called into court. I gave the PC my school photo and it was shown to everyone.

'How old were you when this was taken?' the judge asked.

'I'm wearing my middle-school uniform and so I must have been about nine or ten,' I answered.

Her barrister sat silent. I was half-expecting mine to jump up and say something about me not being a liar, but he didn't.

I was in court for just a short time. Her barrister went over a few things and I was then allowed to go. At last it's all over, I thought to myself. I put my head into the witness room and got Darren's attention. As we left the room we noticed the usher coming up the corridor. She was calling Anthony in. As I walked down the corridor I turned round and saw my brother walking towards the courtroom. I'm sorry, Anthony, I thought. I knew what he was heading for. That was the last time I saw him.

As we left the building we saw Kim, whose mum had just dropped her off. She was going to be called in after Anthony.

Kim asked if I was OK.

'I'm fine,' I told her. I couldn't tell her anything else, as it would put the whole case in jeopardy. 'I just need to get home. Good luck and I'll see you later.' I wanted to stay with Kim, otherwise she would be sitting there by herself, but she wouldn't hear of it.

'How about if Darren sat with you?' I asked.

'No, I'll be fine now. Just go.'

'All right. I'll see you later then.' And with that I left.

We drove home. I didn't have any sense of achievement like I'd felt after my dad's case, but I was extremely happy that at last it was all over. Kim called me later that afternoon to tell me that she wouldn't be coming back to my place tonight, as she needed to take her mum to court. Her mum had been called to give evidence. The PC was on her way round to her house now to get a statement. Kim had been questioned about the tape and had told the court that her parents had also heard it, which was why her mum was needed. It must have strengthened our case to actually have an adult witness.

'I'll see you tomorrow then, Kim,' I said.

I spent the evening very upset. And I'd thought that I'd be dancing round the living room once this one was over, but I wasn't. I felt that I had lost it. Why couldn't I say the things that were in my mind, like I'd done with my dad's case? Maybe it wouldn't have made any difference. I'll never know. At least it was all over. All I had to do now was wait for the verdict.

Kim came back the next day. I was glad to have someone to talk to about it. I couldn't really talk to Darren because he never knew my stepmother, although I'd told him everything about her. I felt that he wouldn't be able to totally believe just how terrifying she was unless he'd seen her in action; or seen that look in her eyes that made your whole body tremble with fear. Kim told me that she was shocked when she first saw my stepmother. She also said that she had noticed that she hadn't changed at all. The PC rang me on the Wednesday to tell me that the proceedings had ended early that day because the defence was calling in another witness. I asked her how Anthony got on.

'He did brilliantly,' she replied. 'He was a bit shocked when he first saw her but after he had a little break he was fine. I'll call you tomorrow then.'

'OK. Bye.'

She rang me early the following afternoon.

'Who was the witness?' I immediately asked.

'Mrs Johnson,' she replied. 'She told the court that you were treated no differently from your brothers and if you were naughty then you got a smack, and that was it. As you had already said that nobody else saw the incidents, she was really just wasting her time. Anyway the jury is out now, so as soon as I hear I'll let you know.'

'Thanks,' I said.

'Well, who was it?' Kim asked.

'Mrs Johnson,' I replied. I was hurt. Her entire family had known all about my stepmother and what she was capable of. Why did she say that? The feeling of 'Oh, it's only Sue' started to sweep over me once again.

My PC rang me again later, but only to tell me that the jury was still out. 'The judge will give them a little more time in the morning and then he will take a majority verdict. So I'll call you in the morning.'

'Could you please tell Kim the news if I don't answer?'

'No problem. Bye.'

I had booked an appointment with the hairdresser. I hadn't been able to get my hair cut for ages and it was now getting out of control. I'd originally thought that everything would be over by Friday.

'So you've had the week off?' the hairdresser asked. 'Done anything exciting?'

'No, not really,' I answered, hoping that she would hurry up as I wanted to get out and see if there had been any news.

Kim was waiting for me in her car. I looked at her and she nodded. I got to the car and she told me that she would tell me what was said as soon as we got home.

'OK,' I said. I lived about a minute's drive away from the hairdresser's and as soon as we got in the door I jokingly screamed, 'Tell me!'

'Well, she's been found guilty on four of the charges. The three sex-abuse charges were all "not guilty" and the "teatime rules" one was also "not guilty".'

I think that Kim thought that I'd be disappointed, but I wasn't. The sex-abuse charges, I felt, might have been put in doubt over my mistake or maybe the jury didn't believe me: whatever their reasoning, I have to accept that she was found not guilty and this is what she must be considered. I thought back to when I was making my statement and how I wasn't going to mention them anyway. Maybe if I hadn't, then the CPS might not have given the go-ahead and we wouldn't have even got to court. The PC rang me. She told me that the jury may have decided that the 'teatime rules' were just normal chastisement.

'I feel sorry for all their kids then,' I told her. I asked her if, when she next spoke to Anthony, she could tell him thanks and that I love him.

'No problem. If he wants to contact you I'll tell him to call me and I'll pass on any message. Sometimes all people need is a little time. Also, I'm sending you down some forms from the Criminal Injuries Board. You may be able to claim some compensation from them.'

'OK. Thanks,' I said.

At last I felt that it was all over. This is it now: I can really start to enjoy the rest of my life. She'll be sentenced in four weeks' time but I don't really care what punishment she gets.

I wrote to my current counsellor and told her that it was all over. I had applied to become a volunteer for Childline but wanted to do more, and could she point me in the right direction? She sent back some information and also an appointment for our next session.

The PC sent me the forms but I didn't have a clue about filling them in, so I rang my local victim support team, who sent a lady round to help me. I was now starting to get back into a routine and was looking forwards, positively, and not backwards. Little things would happen that would remind me of the family. I had to just 'get over it'.

A few weeks later I heard from the PC, who said that the sentencing had been cancelled for another two weeks.

I wasn't bothered as I didn't really care about her sentencing.

On the day the sentence was handed down, 22 March, a Friday, I went to work as normal. I had confided in a workmate, who told me that I should just ring the court to find out what time the sentencing would take place.

'If you don't, then you'll be a nervous wreck all day,' she said.

I rang them and was told that sentencing was scheduled for

three that afternoon. I wanted to be at home when I heard the news and so I finished everything at work and left early. I got home around 3.15. I poured myself a large vodka and Coke and then just sat looking at the phone, waiting for it to ring. Darren had returned from picking up the kids and he sat with me. Just after four the phone buzzed. I had a voicemail message but the phone hadn't even rung. How did it go straight over to voicemail? I wasn't going to waste any time thinking about that, so I pressed the button to listen to the messages. My PC had rung.

'Hi, Sue. Just to let you know that she was given nine months for each guilty charge but it's to run concurrently and has been suspended for two years. What that means is that if she gets into any trouble over the next two years she will have to go to prison to serve her sentence. I'll call you on Monday. Bye.'

So she got off.

I just burst into tears. Tears of anger, frustration and self-pity. I was shocked. She had been found guilty of all the beatings and neglect but she had escaped custodial punishment.

'What was the point?' I kept saying to myself. I had set out to prove that they shouldn't have treated me the way they did but now it felt like she had been given the OK for her actions. I was so distraught. I couldn't stop crying and drank a huge amount in a small space of time. I phoned and texted everyone that I knew and they all said nearly the same thing, that she was a lucky bitch to escape prison. I went to bed. It was only 6.30 but I didn't want the kids to see me in this state. Even though it wasn't meant to be me versus her, it felt like it was and I had lost. I so hate losing. I pictured her, evil her, at home. She'd probably be breaking open a bottle of champagne, celebrating the fact that it was all over for her.

For the next few days I was very angry. I spoke to the PC and asked her, 'Don't you think it was a waste of time?'

'No, not at all. She still has four convictions,' she replied.

Whoopee bloody doo! I thought to myself.

The judge had told my stepmother that if she'd been found guilty on all charges she would have gone away for a very long time.

I had an appointment to see my counsellor on the Wednesday. I didn't cry, of course, but I was very close to it.

'What was the point?' I kept asking her. I also told her that I'd felt that I'd lost the case, for if she'd been found guilty on the sex-abuse charges she would have definitely gone inside. She told me to have a chat with the PC and see what she had to say.

So I rang her up and asked her. She told me that people find it a lot harder to find a woman guilty of sexual abuse, basically because women are seen as the gentler gender and people just will not believe that a woman can do these things. She told me that I didn't do badly and it was an extremely hard case. I did feel a little better, only a little, though. I could have said everything right in court and maybe she still would have been found not guilty.

Next time I saw Susan I told her what the PC had said. She told me that I had placed a brick on a small wall. Other people would come along with their bricks and eventually the wall would be so big that people would be unable to ignore it any more.

I wrote to the District Crown Prosecutor and asked them what was the point of reporting crimes when, even after they are found guilty, they are still allowed to carry on as normal. I also asked them about other children who may be in contact with her. Do their parents not have the right to know what this woman is capable of doing? I got a reply. Basically they said my dad had caused me the most harm and therefore her sentence was suspended because the judge felt that there were exceptional circumstances in this case. Also, if she were to mistreat another child she would then have to go to prison and serve her sentence.

What about the poor child splattered all over the floor? I thought to myself. I still couldn't let it go.

Now I wanted to know exactly what the judge had actually said to them when passing sentence. I wrote to the court reporters and asked them how I could get hold of the court transcripts. I didn't want the whole court cases, just the last bit, the sentencing. I was curious to know what everyone else had said about me in court. I suspected that it wasn't very nice and that I'd rather not know. It would have only made me angrier. My mate Wendy had also enquired about getting the transcripts from her court case and was told that the cost was £100 plus VAT for every recorded hour. So I was very surprised when they arrived on my doormat a few days later without any mention of paying for them. I read them. Once again, seeing it in black and white made it seem so real. When my dad received his six-year sentence, it emphasised just how serious his crime was, which is why I was really taken aback when she was let off and didn't even have a fine to pay. The woman made my life hell, not only when she lived with us, but for years after.

OK. If the courts aren't going to do it, I'll do it myself, I thought. I did have every intention of just sitting outside her house. She would then know that I knew where she lived. People had told me that they would willingly go round and 'have a chat with her'. At first I thought this sounded like a good idea but then I realised that it wasn't the answer. I didn't want her beaten up. I wanted her to realise what she had done and how it had affected me. I think that both she and my father had excused their actions, probably blaming the circumstances instead of themselves.

I made an appointment to see a solicitor. They were very keen to start suing, especially when I told them that my dad owned his own home and it was probably worth about £220,000.

'We'll give you a no-win, no-fee deal,' the solicitor said. 'Look at it this way: you've probably been written out of his will by now, so why not get what's yours?'

I didn't want that. I didn't want Ela – and I think Steven, his wife Nita and their new child were also living there – to become homeless. I had told the PC while making my statement that I would not be suing or looking to gain financially. I never wanted other people – the family, that is – to use the excuse 'Oh, that's why she did it, to get Dad's cash.' Also, my dad was in prison. If it was me I'd be looking forward to getting out, but what would he be looking forward to if I took his home away? No, I didn't want to sue my dad. If I did, then whatever I'd spend the money on would be a constant reminder.

I went to the solicitor with a glimmer of hope that we could go after her and make her sweat it out. I did a search on her home and found that she co-owned it with a housing association; probably a similar scheme to mine and Darren's.

'We'll get both of them,' he said, 'and the good thing is that you've already done most of the work by proving their guilt.'

I said goodbye and told him that I'd have a think about it and let him know. I already knew, though, this wasn't what I wanted. It seemed more like petty revenge than justice.

I then tried to get in touch with two of the national newspapers. I sent them a couple of emails but they never replied. Apparently it's just another child-abuse case. There are so many of them now that it won't reach the headlines unless it's a famous person, which is a pity as I really believe that if I'd known there were other people just like me I would have sought help a lot sooner. I was very, very lucky that I had a husband who has to be the most patient man ever. If he hadn't been so patient another family would have been destroyed. Between us we managed to stop the destructive cycle.

NINETEEN

My first memories of drinking were when I was lying in bed listening to the Evans family across the road or the Johnsons downstairs enjoying themselves. There was a lot of laughter going on. When I was 11 my dad encouraged me to drink. He would give me, not charge me for, drinks and cigarettes. I thought that they would make me look tough and be like an adult and so I willingly took them. What child doesn't take the gifts that their parents offer? My dad passed on his useful tips to me. For instance, if you stood an empty bottle upside down overnight, by morning the lid would be full of vodka, although you had to be very careful unscrewing it so that none got spilled. By the age of 18 I was most definitely an alcoholic. I could never have just one or two but had to get completely plastered. Unfortunately I saw it as an escape from my normal life, even if it was only for a few hours.

During my pregnancies and while I was breastfeeding I

didn't drink. Just typical of me: I will do anything for anyone else but not do anything for myself.

When the children were younger and I was doing the leaflet job I would only have a drink if I had a night off. I would look forward to these nights as they didn't happen very often, maybe once a fortnight. It was my dad who got me the leaflet job. Whatever he got, Ela and I split it 50/50, and so if I had a night off that meant Ela did as well, which would mean one day's less pay coming into the house.

After I found my mum and suddenly realised things weren't quite all right, I drank even more. During my drunken state I could shrug and say, 'Fuck them all.'

When I returned to work I now had every night available to drink as well as the money to pay for it. At first it didn't start off like that. Friday night was always my night but, although I never saw it at the time, every night became Friday night. It just happened. I don't know when, but all of a sudden I was drinking every single day. I had always despised alcoholics. I used to think that they were weak and now I was one. I had always thought, I'll never be that dependent on alcohol, I'm just drinking because I enjoy it and it relaxes me. I was now waking up in the morning and rushing through my day so that I could start drinking. Every single day that I took off sick was due to alcoholism.

After moving out of London I was very lucky to be registered with a great doctor. My London doctors were OK but you rarely saw the same one twice as they were always moving on. When he sent me to my addictions counsellor, Susan, she tried to steer me off my addiction. I knew what I had to do but really just didn't want to do it. I loved my 'don't care' stage and wished that I could be like that 24 hours a day.

I tried to quit many times. I would have my 'last night', when I would drink as much as possible because I would definitely be quitting this time. I would be so determined but after just one sober day I would go back to my friend the bottle. He could stop all my nightmares and make things all right.

My doctor did a blood test on me so that he could check my internal organs. The results came back and they were all clear. He was quite surprised as I had told him that I had been drinking a bottle of vodka a day for months now, maybe even years.

'You're very lucky,' he told me. 'Don't waste this opportunity.'

Susan had told me about this new wonder pill that would make me stop drinking. If you tried to drink while taking it you would be violently sick. George Best was also on these tablets and so that was it: I was most definitely an alcoholic.

I started to take the tablets every day. Even if I missed one day it wouldn't matter, because the tablet would remain in my blood for a week. Every time I took a tablet it meant a sober week lay ahead. I took them for three weeks but hated it. I hated myself for taking them as I was now the one who was preventing me from doing what I really wanted to do. I didn't have anything to look forward to at the end of a hard day's work. So I stopped taking them and went back to drinking. I didn't tell my family at first, because I wanted them to be happy, and so I sneaked my vodka in. Many a time I sat in Tesco's car park with a bottle of vodka, poured it into my Buxton water bottle and threw the empty bottle into the recycling bin.

In both court cases, during which I went through the most horrendous time of my life, I stood up in court sober. When I gave birth and suffered the most immense pain ever, again I was sober. During my counselling I had been on the wagon for ten weeks. It seems obvious that I don't need alcohol to make it through the day. In fact, being an alcoholic has prevented me from living my life to the full. I would love to go swimming, play tennis, generally be more active, and would also love to travel. However, being an alcoholic has made me obese and very unfit. Also, we don't have the money to spare to go travelling.

TWENTY

Today is 15 July 2003, my thirty-fifth birthday. I am sitting here thinking back over the years. I remember receiving my tennis rackets. That year Anthony got an electric organ for his birthday, Andrew got a blue Grifter bike and Paul got a video game. I had by far the best gift, even though they never quite survived the six-week summer holiday. I remember my twelfth birthday, when my dad put a £5 note in my card and wrote in brackets, 'Buy a bra.' I thought it was his shy way of telling me that I needed one. I soon realised that it wasn't when he asked me to show him what it looked like on me.

On my thirteenth the school sent me to 'child guidance' to try to calm me down. My very first session was on that day and I still remember my dad telling me that they were just busybodies sticking their noses in. Most of my birthdays, even when I was very young, were often spent thinking about my mum: my real mum. If there was any day that she was ever going to contact me, I felt that it would be on this day. I tried to look forward to my birthdays but knew that disappointment would most definitely await me. Even after the second post had come I would try to cheer myself up by thinking that it might have been delayed and could arrive tomorrow. The card never came but I was so hopeful that she would at least spend some of the day thinking about me. Mother's Day was also a time when I would constantly think about her.

Karen once did me a Mother's Day card but instead of 'Mother's' she put 'Sister's'. I still have it, along with the first card that she sent to Father Christmas. We would always play I Spy or 'I went to the shop' when we were in our beds.

One night I had a Mars Bar and on her go Karen said, 'I went to the shop and ate Sue's Mars Bar' while taking a mouthful. She nearly choked from laughing so much. Whenever I think of my little sister I will think of those times.

There was my twentieth, when I invited the guys from work home. That was when I first noticed Darren. Just one year later I was pregnant and living in a B&B, but I was still hopeful that I would get my birthday card.

By my twenty-fifth birthday I had come to terms with the fact that my mother was never, ever going to contact me. It didn't matter. I had Sophie, James and Darren. They bought me a cake and put some candles on it: my very first birthday cake.

On my twenty-eighth I finally got my card, but it didn't really mean as much as I'd thought it would.

My thirtieth and I'd just gone back to work. I was very anxious about turning 30 and kept thinking to myself, Should I now start acting like an adult?

Thirty-three and Dad's case should have been starting the next day.

I am now 35 years old. I went to the doctor yesterday for a blood-pressure check and after over two years it's finally down to normal. Phew!

I received £8,200 from the Criminal Injuries Board. It was awarded to me for the abuse I had received from my father but not a penny was awarded for the physical abuse that I got from my stepmother. Again, it seemed like it was unimportant. We spent the money on a few home repairs and paid for a holiday, which we all felt we definitely needed. However, two months later we had to cancel our holiday, as I was made redundant. My mailing company had closed. The internet company offered to keep me on, but at £5,000 a year less and I would have to work an extra ten hours a week. I thought about their kind offer for about 30 seconds and said, 'No, thank you.'

I did stay there for four weeks, though, until I found another job. I now work for a local food company. It's not a job I particularly enjoy doing; it's just a wage and that's it. I have, however, decided that I can't spend the next 30 years of my life doing this and so I looked in the local papers and noticed a few job advertisements for careers in working with children. I wrote to the name at the bottom of the advertisement and told him that, although I haven't any qualifications, I would love a career in this field and could he please advise me of the best route to take? He actually came round to my home and we had a good long chat. He told me of a few local centres that could use volunteers, and then at least I would have some experience.

So I have decided to become a child mentor. I have now

been trained and have actually just received a call from my supervisor telling me that they have matched me up with a 13-year-old boy. My job as a mentor is to gain the child's trust, listen to them, understand them and not exert any authority over them but try to steer them away from the 'wrong route'. I think it's a great idea.

I do sometimes wonder why I never took to a life of crime when I had the hallmarks of a seriously troubled adolescent. Where did I get my caring nature? It certainly wasn't from my parents.

Darren and I attended our children's open evenings last week and most of the teachers said something like: 'They were both a pleasure to teach and a real credit to you.' I was so proud. They are great children and, even though I have to yell at them sometimes to tidy up after themselves, they both have good hearts and care about others.

I then wondered, Who am *I* a credit to? I just have to say that it's me. I was lucky enough to be born with a caring nature. I suppose I could have chosen to ignore it, but for some reason I didn't.

A few weeks ago I heard that my sister Karen had given birth to another little boy. As soon as I heard the news I just burst into tears. It still hurts after two years that I am no longer part of her or her children's lives.

I wrote to my Auntie Hilary. I told her that I had waited for things to calm down before I wrote. Basically I just said, Thanks, and that she was the kindest person, ever, to me. I tried to explain why I did it but couldn't. I just said, 'I had to do it.' I didn't get a reply. I was a bit disappointed and preferred it when I knew that she couldn't contact me rather than wouldn't.

I didn't have a choice. I had to do it. I really did. I have children and they are the most precious things ever. Not just mine, but all kids. The first time I heard the school children sing 'Little Donkey' my eyes filled up with tears. More than once I've been walking round my local supermarket and heard a Tannoy announcement asking some mother to contact customer services as they had her lost child. I just can't help but feel sorry for the little child, and mother, when they suddenly look up and realise that one of them is missing. A couple of times in the past I have grabbed my son's hand and walked away before suddenly looking down and realising that I have hold of someone else's. The child didn't even realise that I wasn't his mother. Scary.

Children are so precious and I really do despise adults who mistreat them. I feel that many people turned a blind eye to the way that little Susan Hamford was treated but I just couldn't do that. I will not accept that are any 'exceptional' circumstances, because there just aren't. Nobody has the right to mistreat a child in the way that they did. And that is why I had to do it. Child abuse is wrong and, even though she never served time in prison, I proved that they were both wrong to treat me, a child, like they did. She is now Deidre Evans, a convicted child beater. They were both guilty of abuse offences. Every child deserves the best start in life.

I do feel a little upset that I've wasted so much of my life worrying about the things that have happened. For the past 20 years I have been ashamed, embarrassed, disgusted with myself and so full of self-loathing. I never liked myself and so I didn't believe that other people could like me. I was deeply embarrassed about my 'secrets', but there were not my fault. If someone slaps you around the face you say, 'Ouch.' If someone tickles your toes you giggle. Sometimes you have no control over your body's reactions. I am, after all, a normal human being.

I read Billy Connolly's book, where he says that he was severely abused by his aunts and sexually abused by his father. But he stated on *Parkinson* that when he thinks of his dad he remembers the good times. This remark kept coming back to me, but no matter how much I tried I couldn't think of any good times with either my dad or my stepmother.

It is very worrying that I 'slipped through the net'. How did a lady give her baby away and nobody said anything? How did a family appear with a baby, change her name and pass her off as their own? How did I get accepted at schools when I didn't have a proper birth certificate? I honestly believe that she could have killed me and nobody would have missed me, as Susan Hamford didn't legally exist. I got through it but the scary thought is: How many children didn't?

I count myself very lucky. I have a great husband, two fantastic children, a lovely home in a beautiful area and the best friends ever. These last two years have been a real eye-opener as to who does and doesn't matter in my life. OK, I lost the Hamford side of the family, but I do have my mother's side. Even though having a mother wasn't as great as I'd always imagined it to be – dreams rarely are – I am still glad that I found her. Apart from her one big mistake, she really is a good person. My three new sisters are great, especially Clare, who has always been there for me. Just like Claudette and Kim have been. Sometimes things have not just crept up on me but landed right on top of me. I have, on many occasions, rung Claudette and Kim, bawling my eyes out. They have all patiently sat and listened to my fears and 'given it to me straight'. I now truly know the meaning of a good friend.

Darren and I are getting on so much better now. We are honest with each other and have spent time with each other, a thing I had previously dreaded. Sometimes my parents' abuse enters my mind but it is becoming a less frequent occurrence and more often than not I can just push it away. I am just so lucky that I have my Darren, who has always stood by me.

I am now looking forward to the rest of my life. I can't change my past: it happened and I have to learn to live with it. Just like I can't change the way the Hamford family feel about me. Even though it hurts and I miss them all, I really don't blame them. It must surely be better to have a mad sister than a perverted father. They all see him as their dad, whereas I see him as a horrible, sweaty pervert, lusting over me – me as a child.

Ela was there that day at court; she heard everything. Deep down she knows the truth. The same as my older brothers; they all know. I still miss them all. Everyday things remind me of them, songs, games and Christmas of course, and I do feel that my dad got six years but I got life. He will be released in October 2005. Things will never be the same again, but I will learn how to live with it.

I will always be grateful to Royal Mail for offering me their Occupational Health service, who then managed to find me a suitable counsellor. Even though I was hurt at the time that they wanted to put me back on the Ops floor, I can now see that a large company has to have procedures and to stick to them.

There is only one person that can change my life and that is me. Being an adult means that you have to make choices and live with them. I have now chosen not to drink and to get back into shape so that I can start to do the things that I previously enjoyed doing. I have even bought a little mirror, just to see how good I look. Shitface no longer exists.

If I had the choice of doing it all again – going to court – I would. Even though I lost my family, and especially my little sister, I would still do it all over again. Child abuse is wrong and ruins lives, not just the victim's life but also those of the victim's spouse and children – it's a never-ending cycle.

I have a key ring which quite simply says: 'Shit happens.' And it does. Sometimes there isn't anything you can do about it. But sometimes there is!